Learn To Tell Time Kindergarten Workbook

Kids Ages 5 – 6

Practice Hours, Half Hours, Quarter Hours, Days and Months with 100+ Activities

Ann K. Bishop

PUZZLE CHEER

EDUCATIONAL RESOURCES

www.puzzlecheer.com

Did your child enjoy this book? Did they have a favorite page or activity?

If so, I'd love to hear about it.

Please share your review so other families can find this book, too.

Every kind review really helps!

Thank you. *Ann K.*

Scan to leave a review.

https://www.amazon.com/review/create-review?&asin=B09DMXTHQP

This workbook belongs to:

_____

· ·

_____

Contents

Analog Clock Introduction

Analog clocks use a clock face to show the time through the use of pointers called hands, numbers, and markings.

hour hand — small hand moves clockwise ↷ to the next hour

minute hand — big hand moves clockwise ↷ to the next minute

hours — numbers
for example — 1 o'clock

minutes — small marks

Digital Clock Introduction

Digital clocks use numbers to show the time. The hours and minutes are separated by a colon :

Examples: 12 o'clock is 12:00
                   1 o'clock is 1:00

12:00

↳ hours

12:00

↳ minutes

Let's Learn The Hours

These are all the hours on the clock. The big hand always points to 12 and the little hand points to the hour number.

Below each clock is the matching digital time.

12:00

1:00

2:00

3:00

4:00

5:00

6:00

7:00

8:00

9:00

10:00

11:00

Name:_____ Date:_____

Practice tracing and writing the time.

twelve

12:00

Draw the
12:00 hour
hand.

Practice tracing and writing the time.

one

1:00

Draw the
1:00 hour
hand.

Name:_____ Date:_____

Practice tracing and writing the time.

two

2:00

Draw the
2:00 hour
hand.

Practice tracing and writing the time.

three

3:00

Draw the
3:00 hour
hand.

Name:_____ Date:_____

Practice tracing and writing the time.

four

4:00

Draw the
4:00 hour
hand.

Practice tracing and writing the time.

five

5:00

Draw the
5:00 hour
hand.

Practice tracing and writing the time.

six

6:00

Draw the
6:00 hour
hand.

Practice tracing and writing the time.

seven

7:00

Draw the
7:00 hour
hand.

Name:_____ Date:_____

Practice tracing and writing the time.

eight

8:00

Draw the
8:00 hour
hand.

Practice tracing and writing the time.

nine

9:00

Draw the
9:00 hour
hand.

Practice tracing and writing the time.

ten

10:00

Draw the 10:00 hour hand.

Practice tracing and writing the time.

eleven

11:00

Draw the 11:00 hour hand.

Name: _____ Date: _____

There are 12 hours on this clock.
Practice tracing the number for each hour.

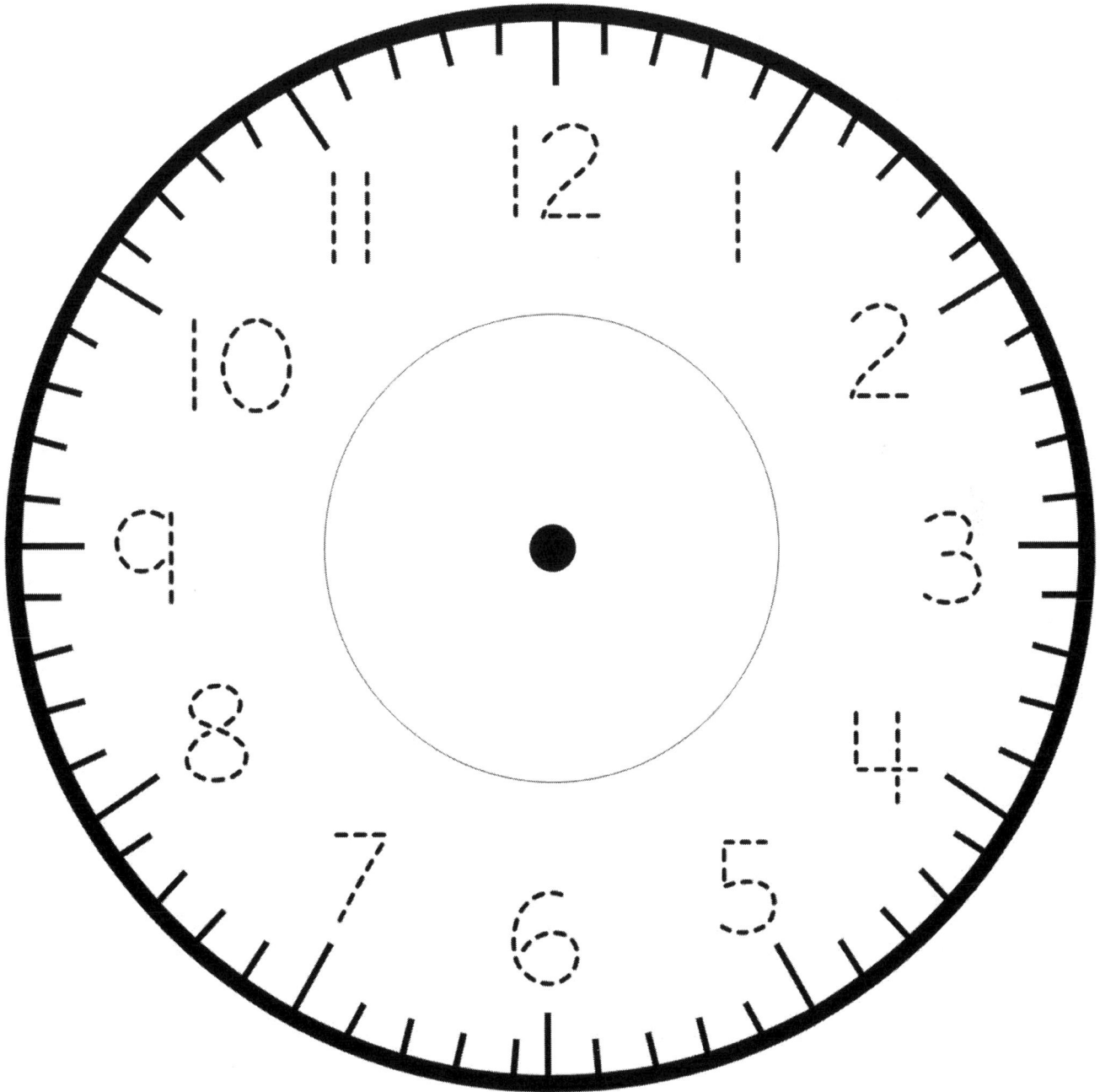

12
11 1
10   2
9   3
8   4
7   5
6

11 12 1
10   2
9   3
8   4
7   5
6

Name: _____ Date: _____

Practice writing the number for each hour.
The first number is traceable for you.

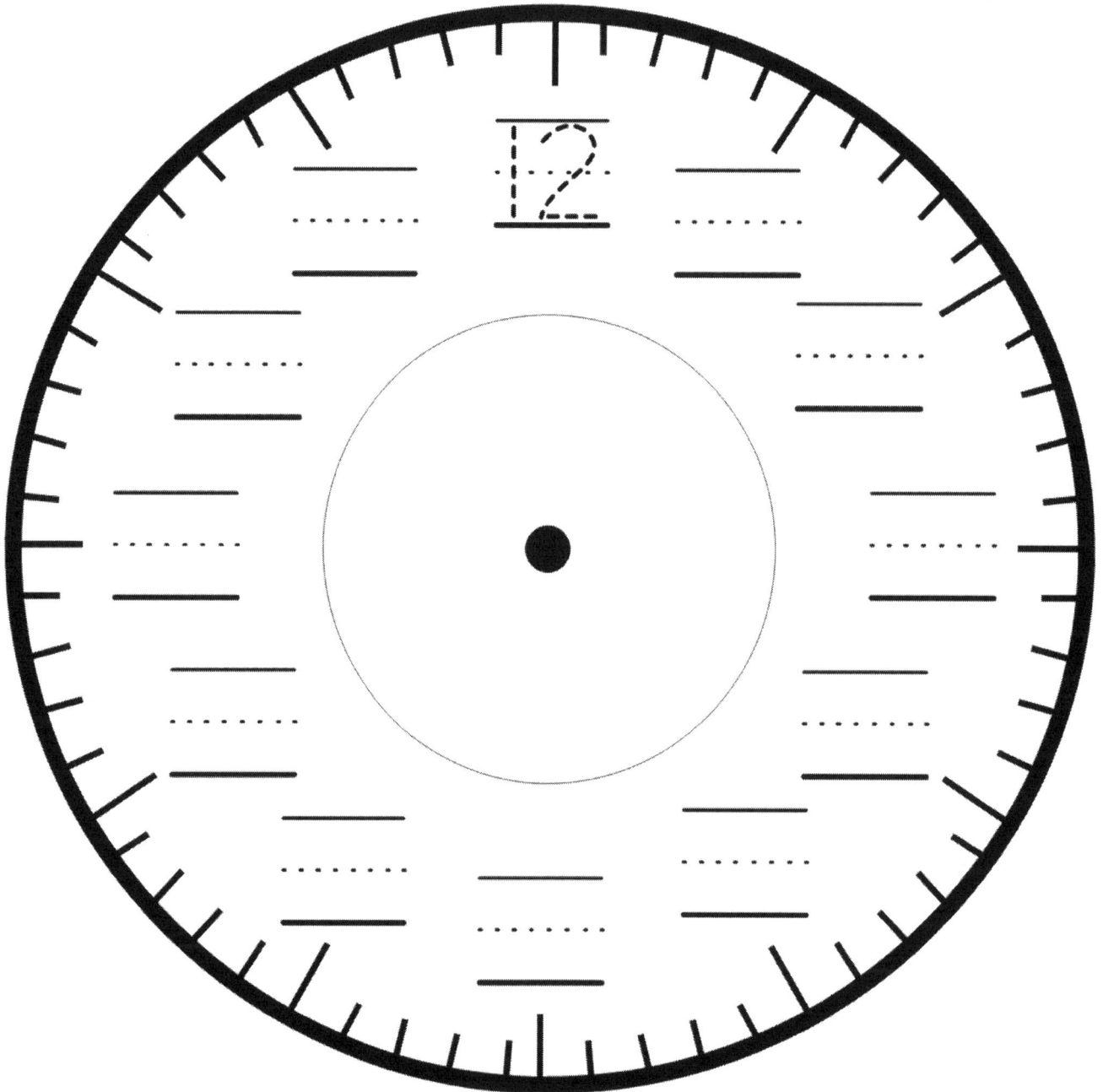

12

Name:_____ Date:_____

Practice tracing the number words on the clock.

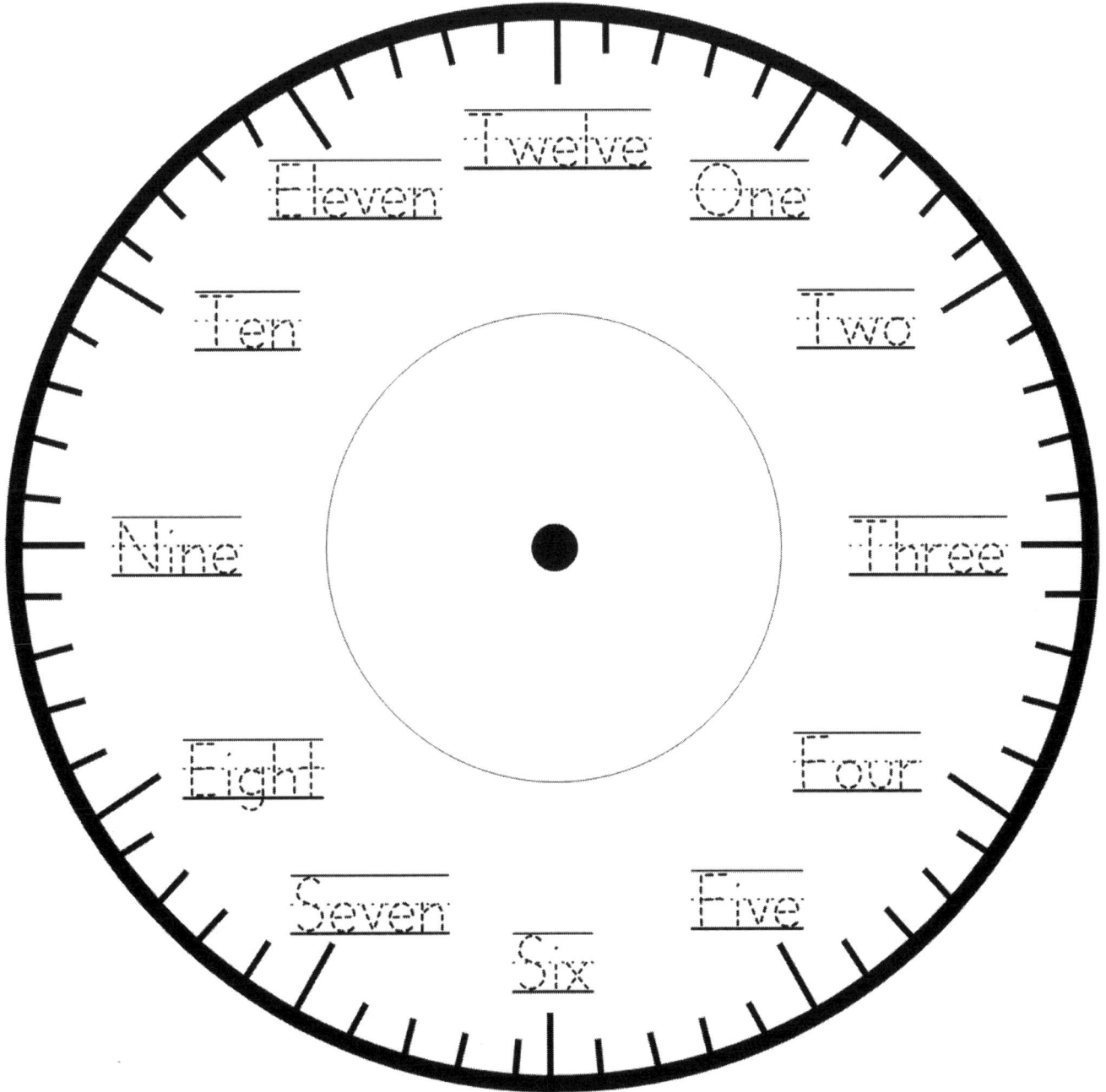

Twelve
Eleven
One
Ten
Two
Nine
Three
Eight
Four
Seven
Five
Six

Name:_____ Date:_____

Practice writing the number word for each hour.
The first number word is traceable for you.

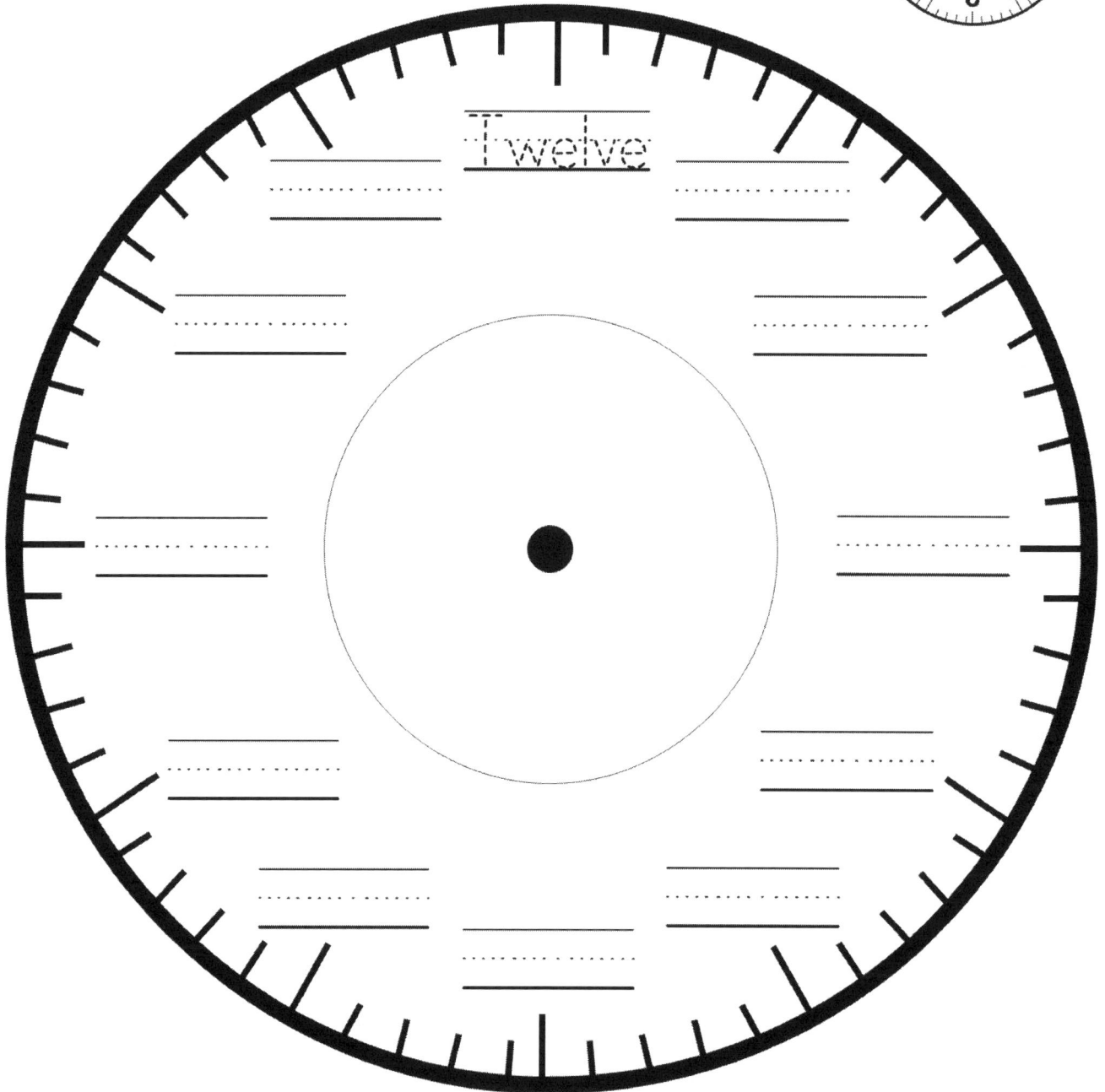

Twelve

Name: _____ Date: _____

Use "o'clock" when there are no minutes.
When it's 1:00 you say: "It's one o'clock."

Practice filling in the clock hands and writing the digital time
for each hour. The first one is filled in for you.

Twelve o'clock

12:00

One o'clock

Two o'clock

Three o'clock

Four o'clock

Five o'clock

Name:_____ Date:_____

Practice filling in the clock hands and
writing the digital time for each hour.

Six o'clock

_____
· · · · · · · · · · ·
_____

Seven o'clock

_____
· · · · · · · · · · ·
_____

Eight o'clock

_____
· · · · · · · · · · ·
_____

Nine o'clock

_____
· · · · · · · · · · ·
_____

Ten o'clock

_____
· · · · · · · · · · ·
_____

Eleven o'clock

_____
· · · · · · · · · · ·
_____

Name: _____ Date: _____

Connect the hours in each maze below.

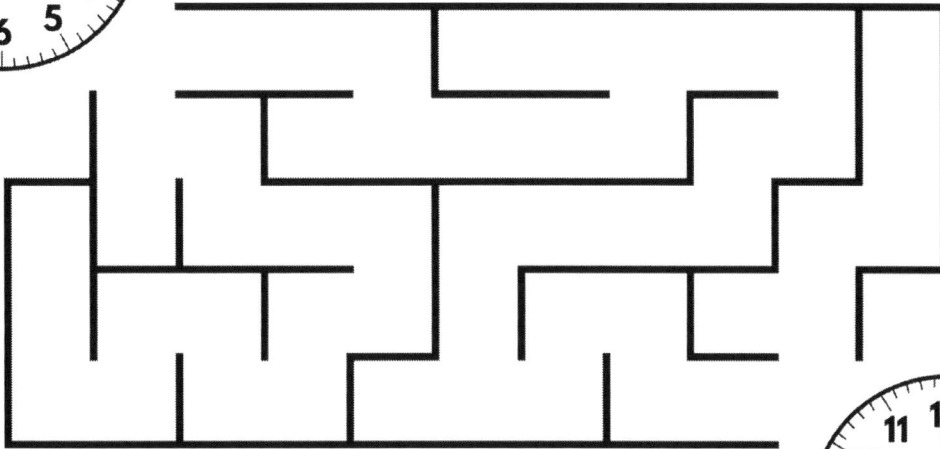

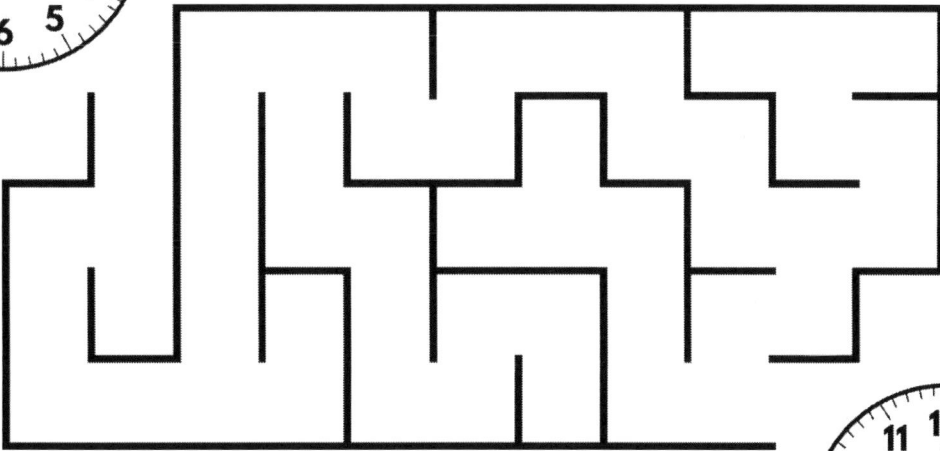

Name: _____   Date: _____

Connect the hours in each maze below.

Name:_____ Date:_____

Connect the hours in each maze below.

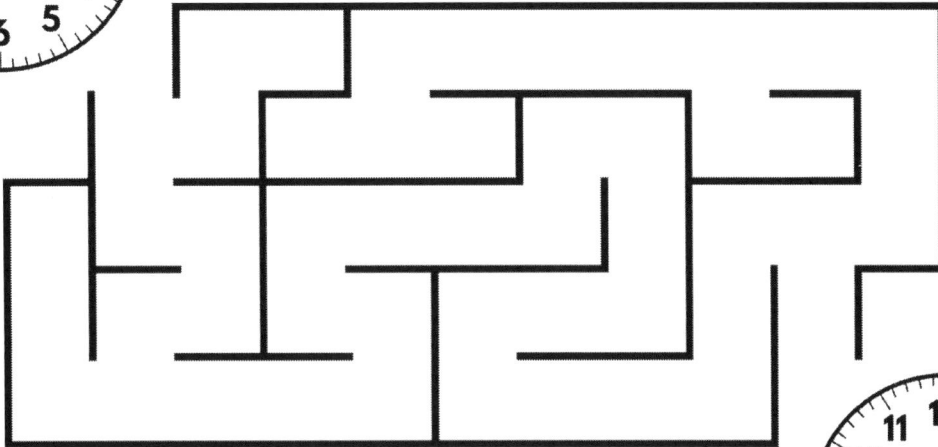

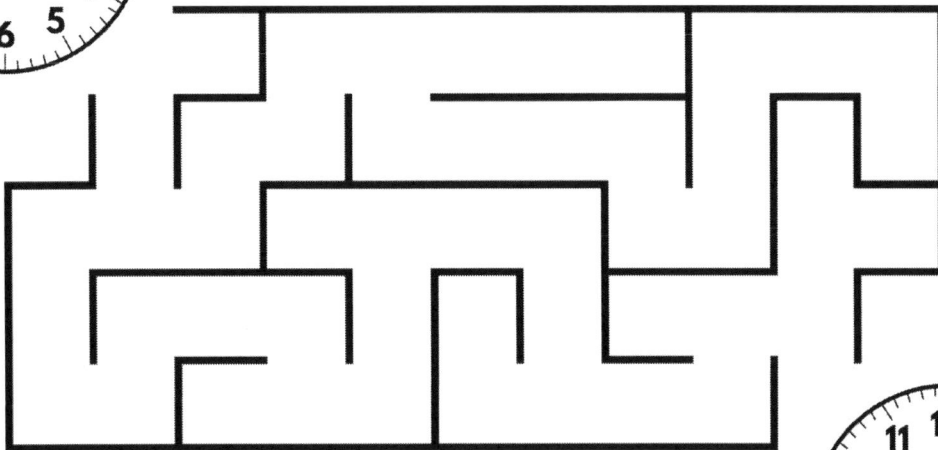

Page 21

Name: _____ Date: _____

Connect the hours in each maze below.

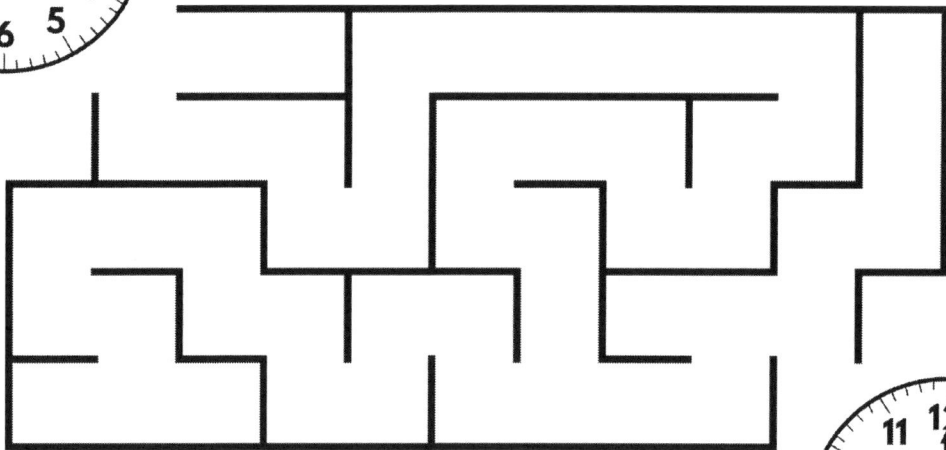

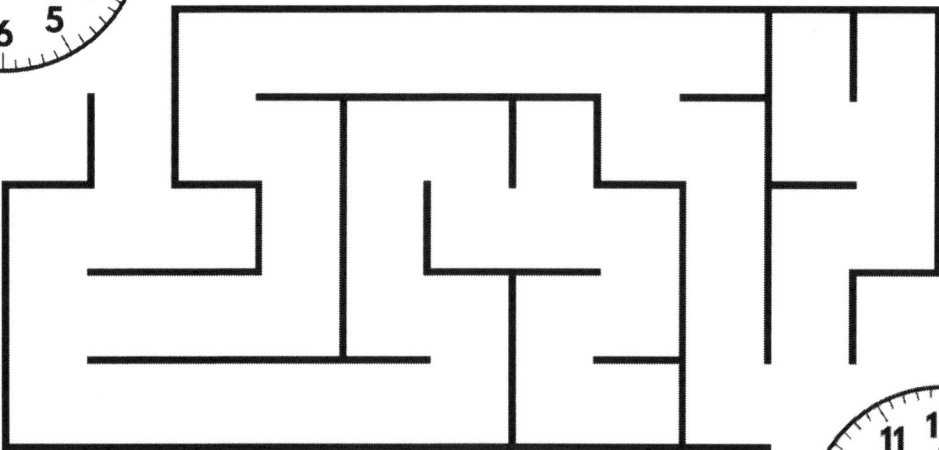

Name:_____ Date:_____

Circle the clock closest to when you wake up.

Circle the clock closest to the time you eat lunch.

Circle the clock closest to the time you go to bed.

Name:_____ Date:_____

Circle the clock closest to the time school starts.

Circle the clock closest to the time school ends.

Circle the clock closest to the time you have a snack.

Page 24

Name:_____ Date:_____

Draw a line to match the clock to the digital time.

 5:00

 4:00

 2:00

 6:00

 1:00

 3:00

Name:_____ Date:_____

Draw a line to match the clock to the digital time.

   **9:00**

   **11:00**

   **7:00**

   **12:00**

   **8:00**

   **10:00**

Name: _____ Date: _____

Draw a line to match the clock to the hour number.

three

four

one

six

two

five

Name:_____ Date:_____

Draw a line to match the clock to the hour number.

ten

twelve

seven

eleven

eight

nine

```
P C K T V O H O X T P T E F H
Z O Q D W V O V J S Z C W O W
E I G H T E W E L E V E N N Z
C M W G N Q L J J T W G K E Y
D Z T M M P H V M E U T M W V
W F K K T S K R E N C L O C K
X Q C W Y S Q P F U T X K Q R
J Y M P G S H O U R S I P K E
J A Z K Q I K Z Y D O Z M G G
I R P O X X Q W P Y P L F E F
S V L N T X D T M V G F I V E
S E H C I W W H O B G Q G R J
L K V L A N O R H X B I Y O O
K L O E F L E E F O U R P N A
A C E A N N B E O S A W K G J
```

CLOCK	HOURS	TEN
EIGHT	NINE	THREE
ELEVEN	ONE	TIME
FIVE	SEVEN	TWELVE
FOUR	SIX	TWO

Let's Learn The Half Hours

When the minute hand is on the 6, the time is 30 minutes after the hour or half past.

Below each clock is the matching digital time.

12:30

1:30

2:30

3:30

4:30

5:30

6:30

7:30

8:30

9:30

10:30

11:30

Name:_____ Date:_____

Trace the digital time and number word that the clock shows.

12:30

Twelve-thirty

Circle the time to match the clock.

10:30

12:30

5:30

Draw the minute hand to show 12:30.

Name:_____ Date:_____

Trace the digital time and number word that the clock shows.

1:30

One-thirty

Circle the time to match the clock.

2:30

8:30

1:30

Draw the minute hand to show 1:30.

Name:_____ Date:_____

Trace the digital time and number word that the clock shows.

2:30

Two-thirty

Circle the time to match the clock.

2:30

1:30

9:30

Draw the minute
hand to show
2:30.

Trace the digital time and number word that the clock shows.

3:30

Three-thirty

Circle the time to match the clock.

10:30

3:30

6:30

Draw the minute hand to show 3:30.

Trace the digital time and number word that the clock shows.

4:30

Four-thirty

Circle the time to match the clock.

1:30

11:30

4:30

Draw the minute hand to show 4:30.

Name:_____ Date:_____

Trace the digital time and number word that the clock shows.

5:30

Five-thirty

Circle the time to match the clock.

5:30

7:30

2:30

Draw the minute
hand to show
5:30.

Trace the digital time and number word that the clock shows.

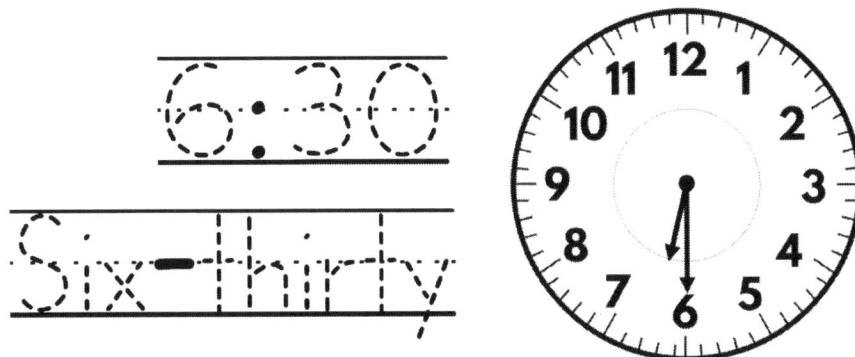

6:30

Six-thirty

Circle the time to match the clock.

6:30

1:30

3:30

Draw the minute
hand to show
6:30.

Name: _____ Date: _____

Trace the digital time and number word that the clock shows.

7:30

Seven-thirty

Circle the time to match the clock.

2:30

9:30

7:30

Draw the minute hand to show 7:30.

© Puzzle Cheer Educational Resources
Page 38

Name:_____ Date:_____

Trace the digital time and number word that the clock shows.

8:30

Eight-thirty

Circle the time to match the clock.

10:30

8:30

6:30

Draw the minute hand to show 8:30.

Name: _____ Date: _____

Trace the digital time and number word that the clock shows.

9:30

Nine-thirty

Circle the time to match the clock.

9:30

7:30

1:30

Draw the minute
hand to show
9:30.

Name: _____ Date: _____

Trace the digital time and number word that the clock shows.

10:30

Ten-thirty

Circle the time to match the clock.

2:30

4:30

10:30

Draw the minute hand to show 10:30.

Name:_____ Date:_____

Trace the digital time and number word that the clock shows.

11:30

Eleven-thirty

Circle the time to match the clock.

10:30

6:30

9:30

Draw the minute hand to show 11:30.

Name:_____ Date:_____

Connect the clocks as they move forward 30 minutes.

12:00

12:30

1:00

1:30

2:00

2:30

Name: Vivia   Date: _____

Connect the clocks as they move forward 30 minutes.

3:00

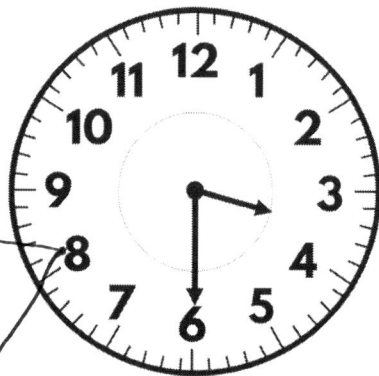
3:30

4:00

4:30

5:00

5:30

Page 44

Name:_____ Date:_____

Connect the clocks as they move forward 30 minutes.

6:00

6:30

7:00

7:30

8:00

8:30

Name:_____ Date:_____

Connect the clocks as they move forward 30 minutes.

9:00

9:30

10:00

10:30

11:00

11:30

Read the clock then trace and write the time.

12:30

1:30

2:30

3:30

Read the clock then trace and write the time.

4:30

5:30

6:30

7:30

Name: _____ Date: _____

Read the clock then trace and write the time.

8:30

9:30

10:30

11:30

Name: Vivia   Date: _____

Circle the clock that matches the number word and digital time.

| Twelve-thirty | 12:30 |

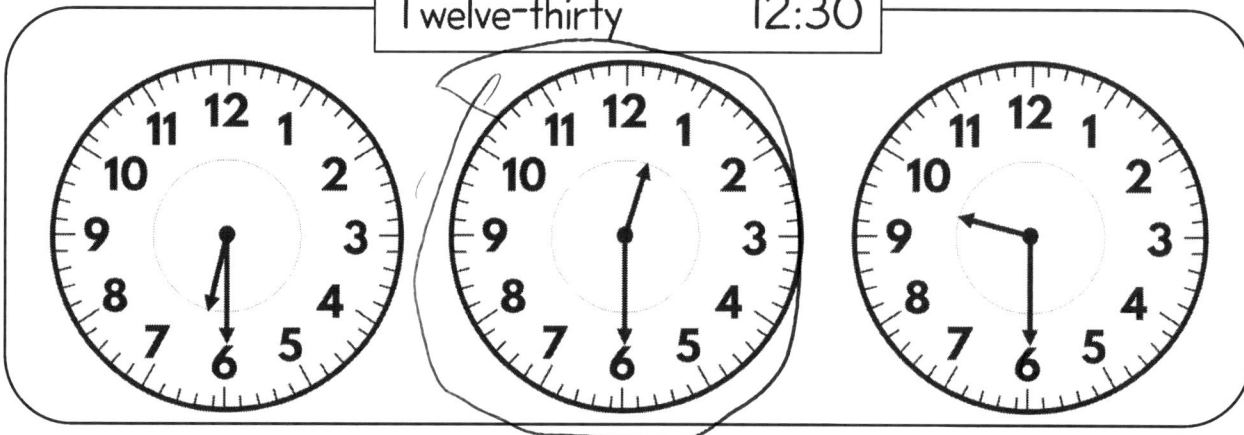

| One-thirty | 1:30 |

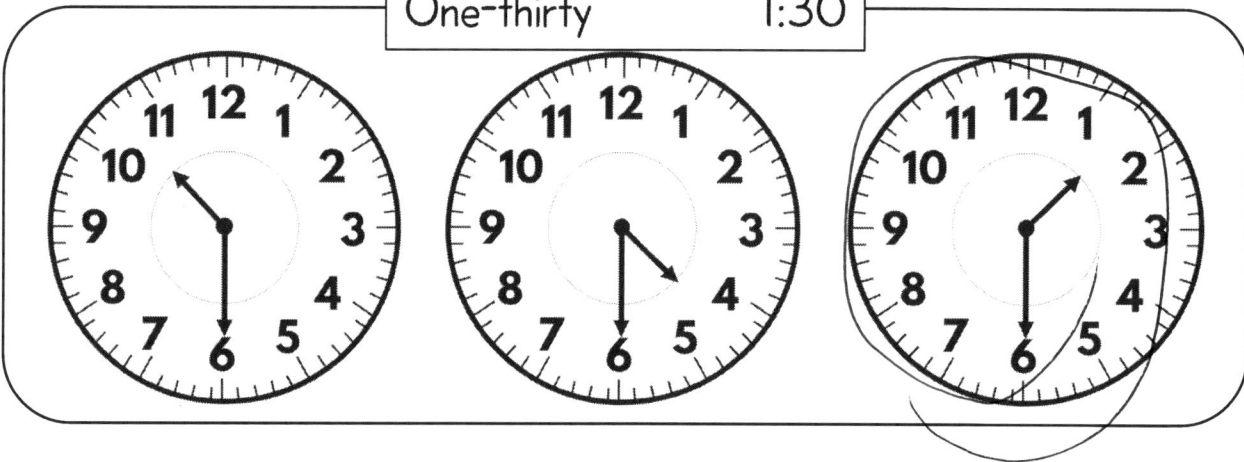

| Two-thirty | 2:30 |

Name: Vivid   Date: _____

Circle the clock that matches the number word and digital time.

Three-thirty   3:30

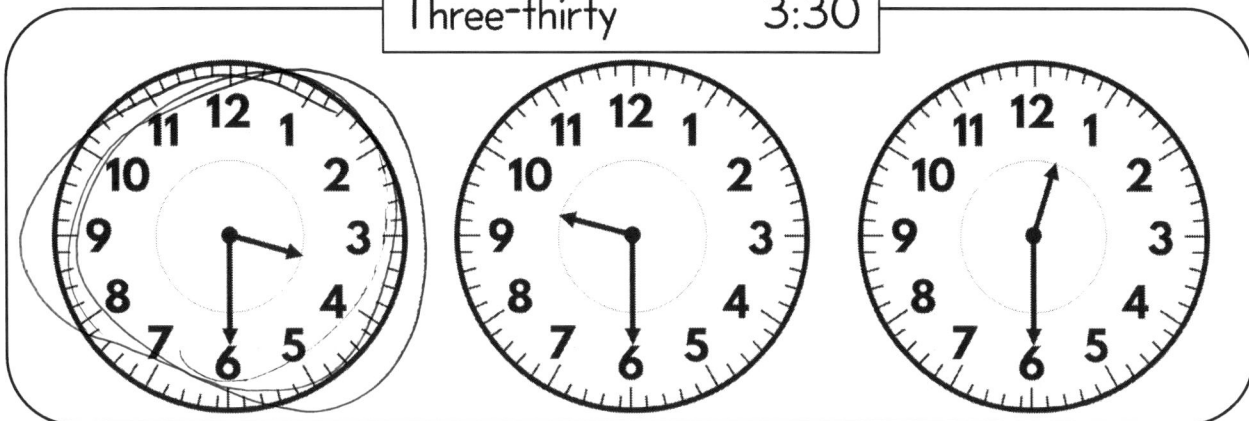

Four-thirty   4:30

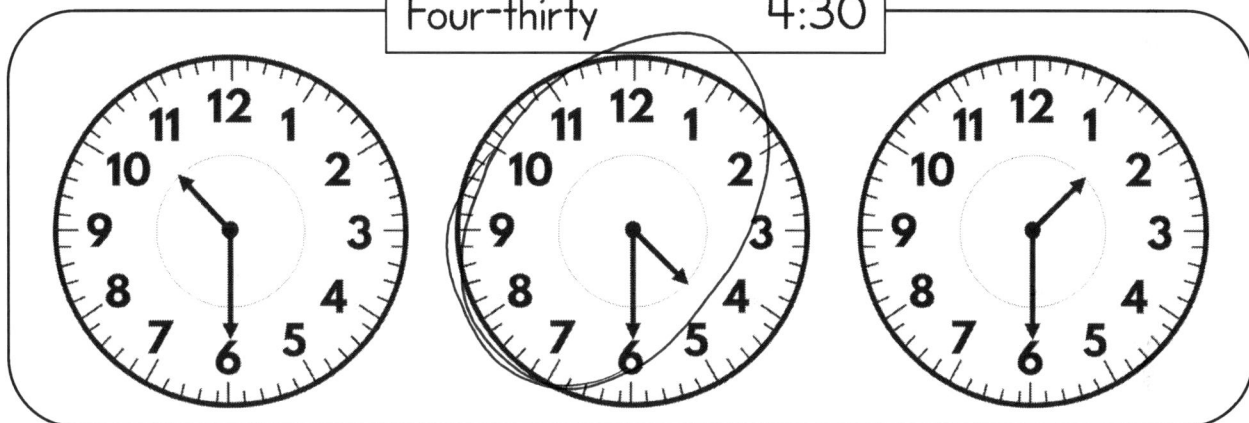

Five-thirty   5:30

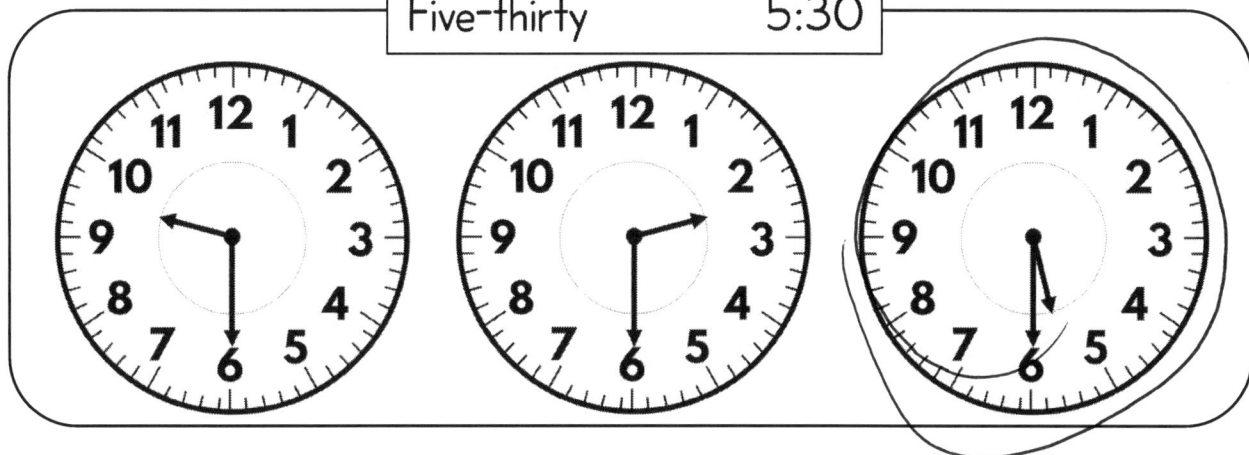

Name:_____ Date:_____

Circle the clock that matches the number word and digital time.

| Six-thirty | 6:30 |

| Seven-thirty | 7:30 |

| Eight-thirty | 8:30 |

Name:_____ Date:_____

Circle the clock that matches the number word and digital time.

| Nine-thirty | 9:30 |

| Ten-thirty | 10:30 |

 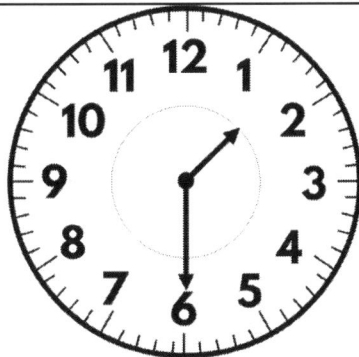 

| Eleven-thirty | 11:30 |

Name:_____ Date:_____

Connect the hour to the half hour in each maze below.

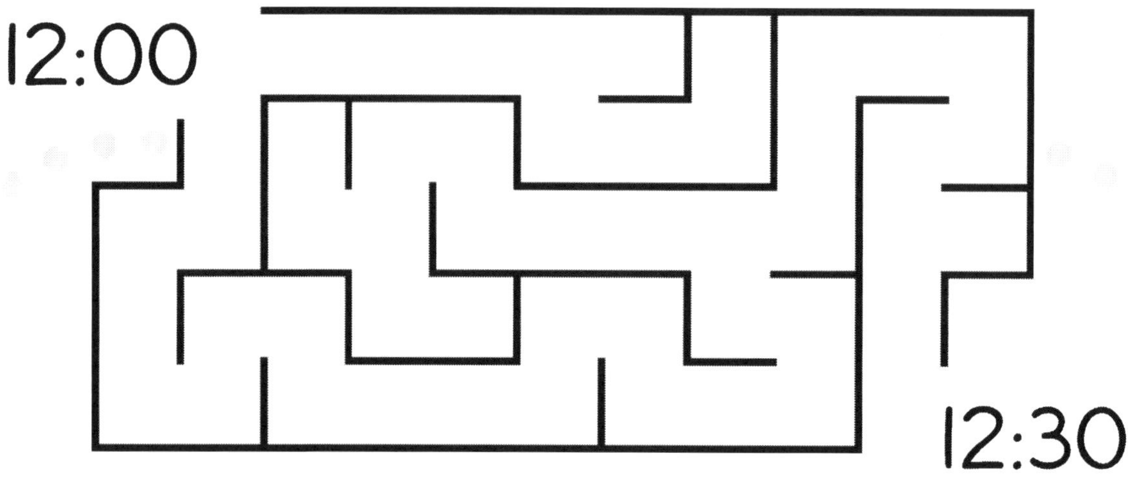

12:00

12:30

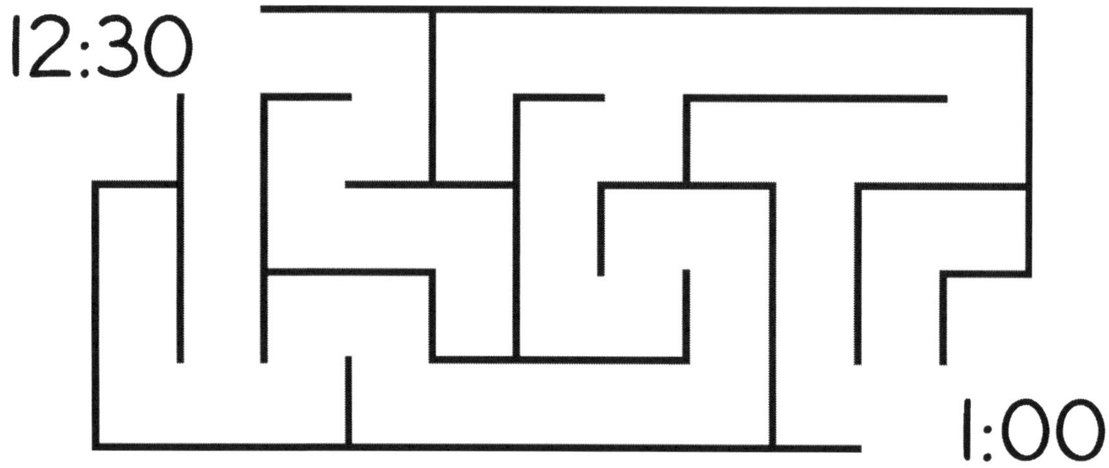

12:30

1:00

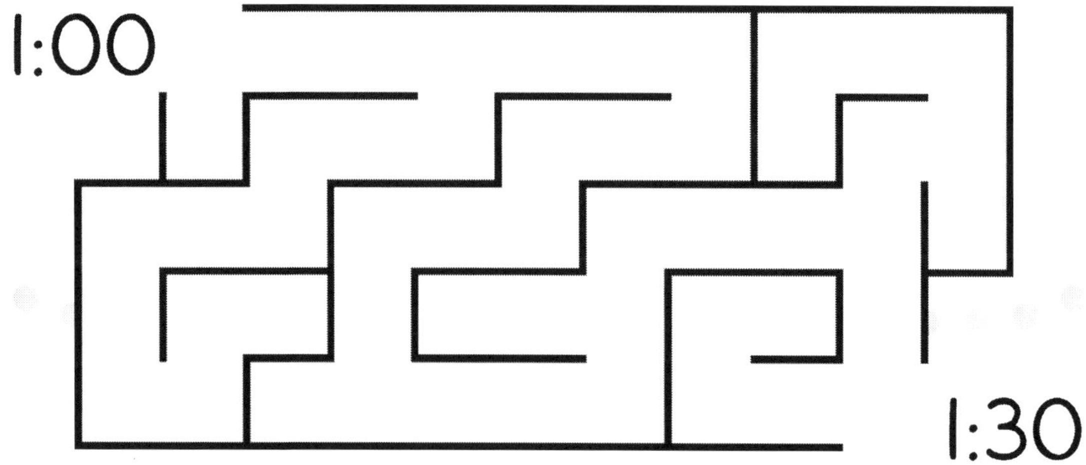

1:00

1:30

Name:_____ Date:_____

Connect the hour to the half hour in each maze below.

3:00

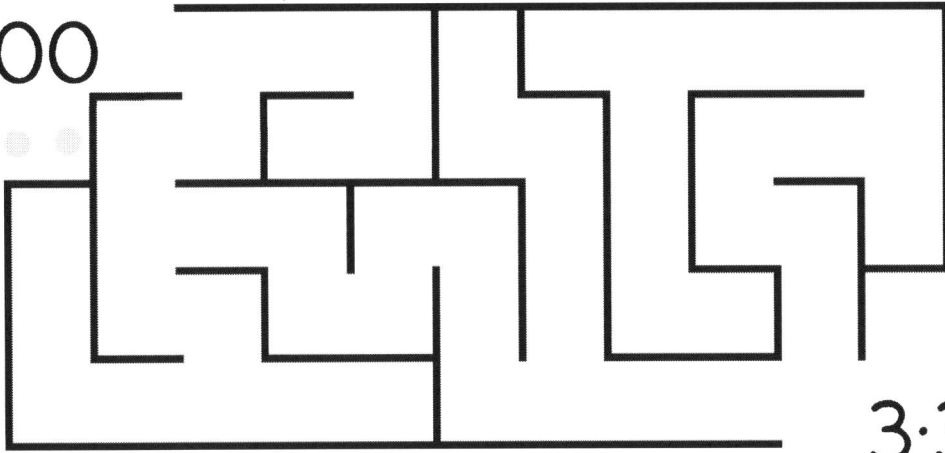

3:30

3:30

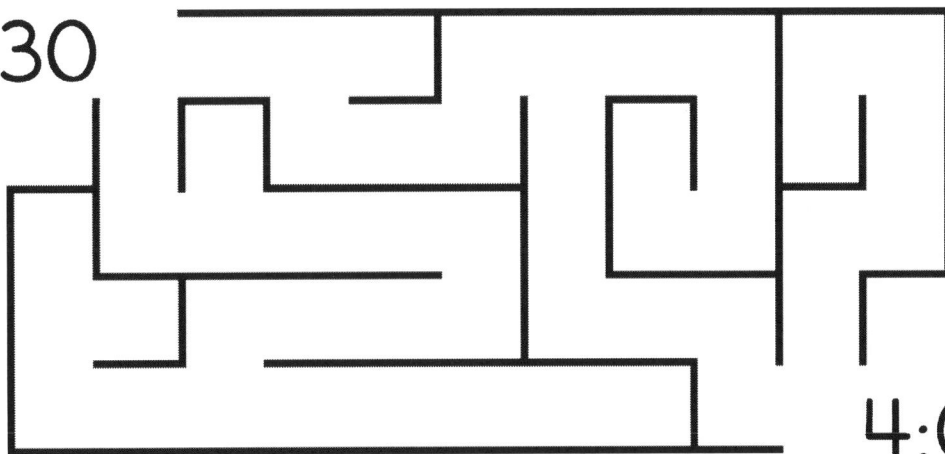

4:00

4:00

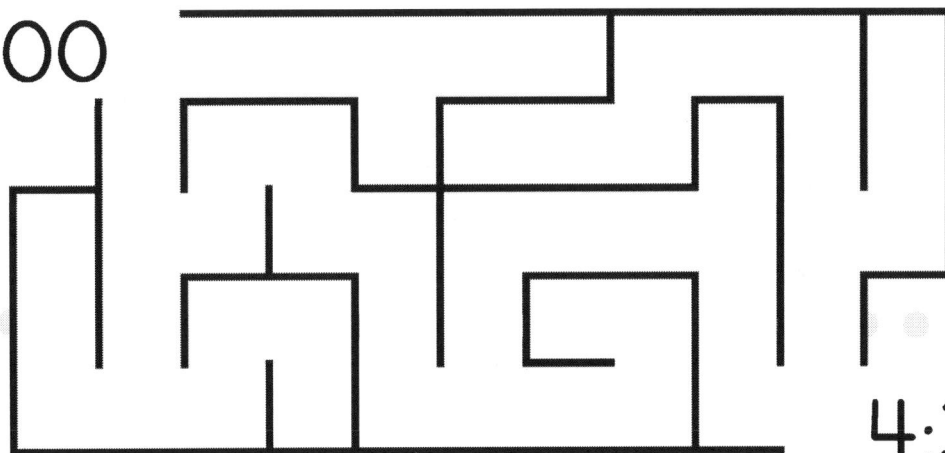

4:30

Name:_____ Date:_____

Connect the hour to the half hour in each maze below.

6:00

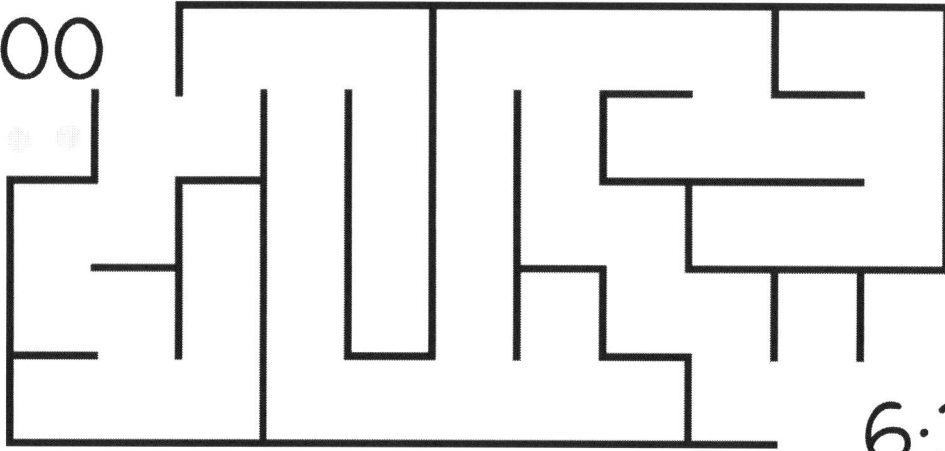

6:30

6:30

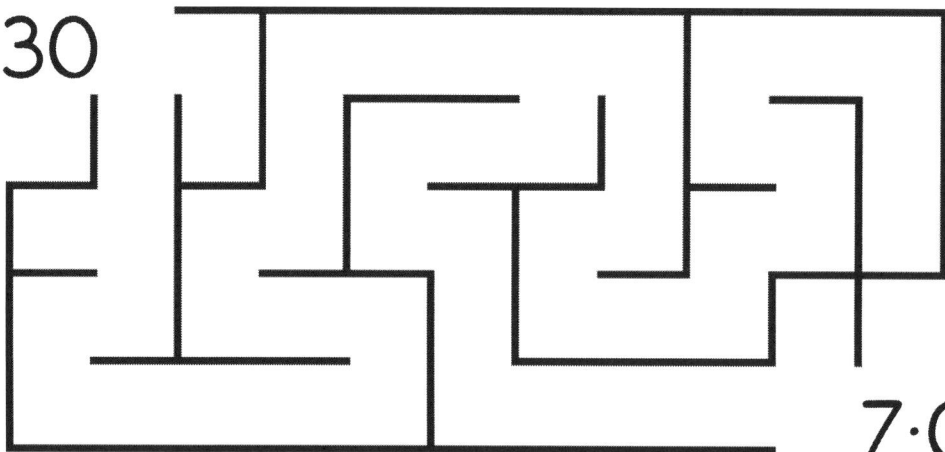

7:00

7:00

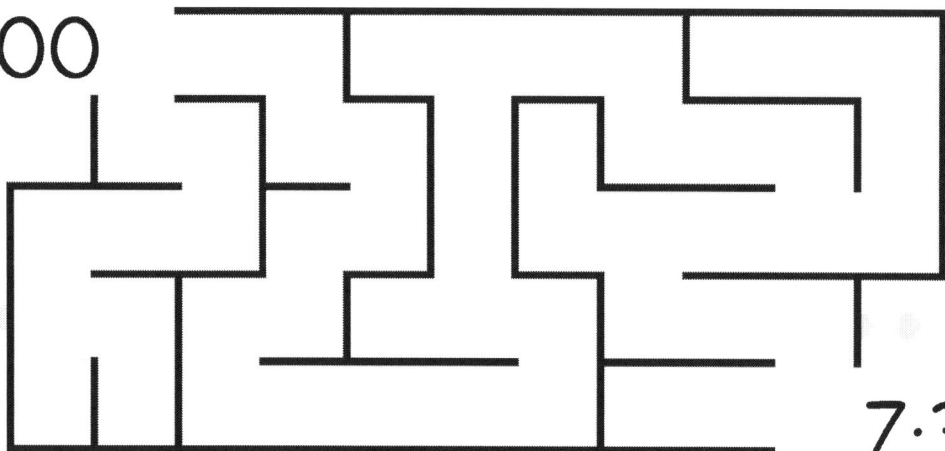

7:30

Name:_____ Date:_____

Connect the hour to the half hour in each maze below.

10:00

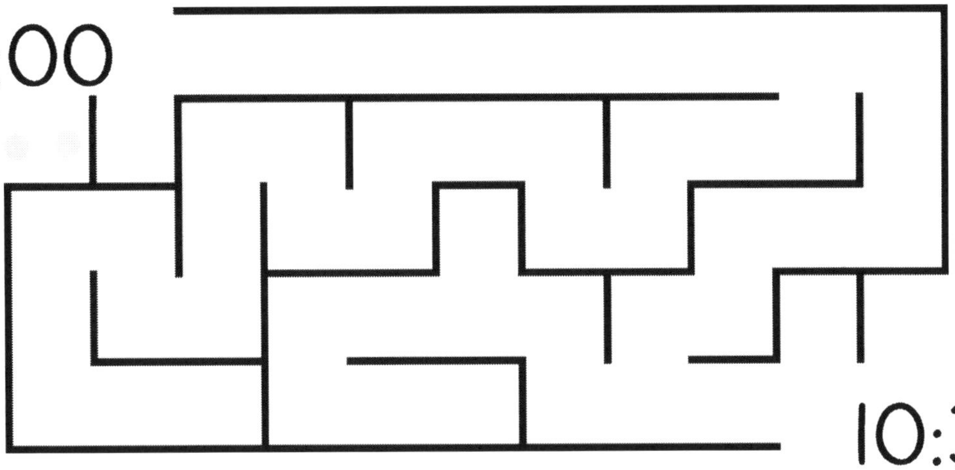

10:30

11:00

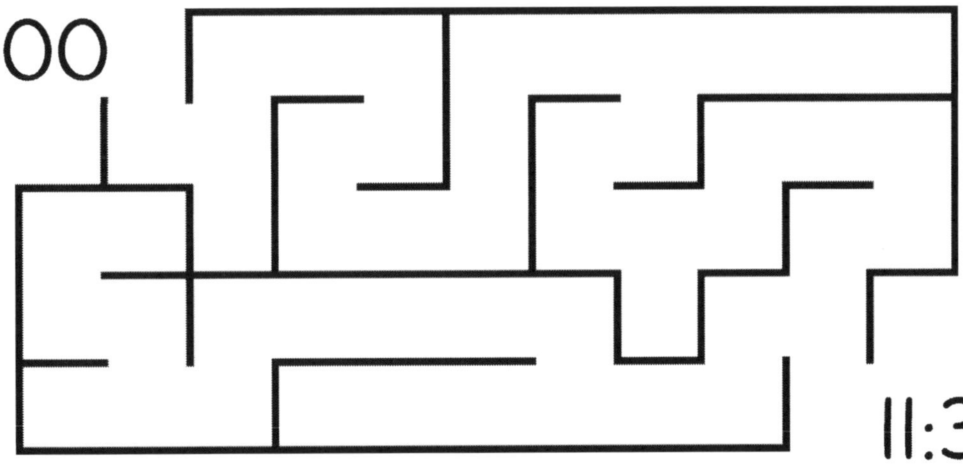

11:30

12:00

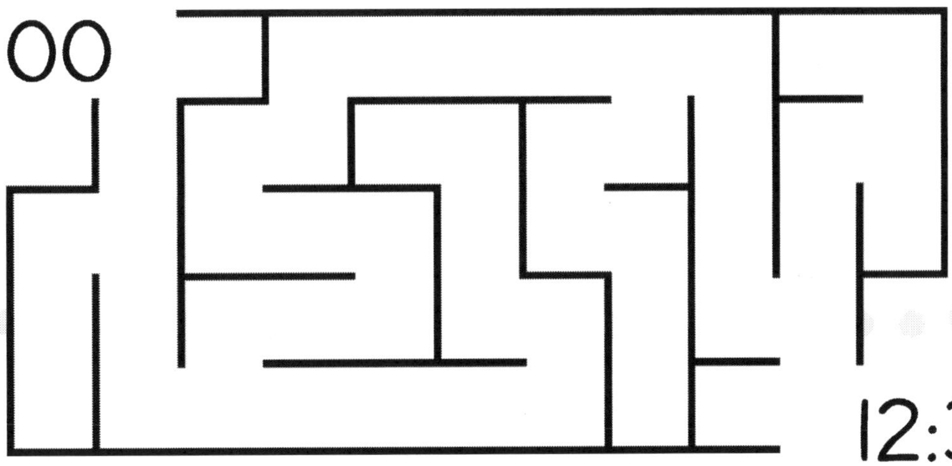

12:30

Name:_____ Date:_____

Draw the minute hand to match the digital time below the clock.

12:00

4:30

7:30

3:00

11:00

9:00

Name:_____ Date:_____

Draw the minute hand to match the digital time below the clock.

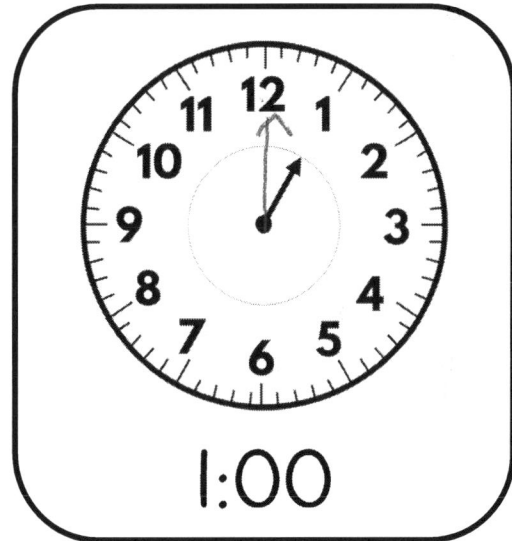

2:30

8:30

6:00

1:00

5:30

9:30

Name:_____ Date:_____

Draw the minute hand to match the digital time below the clock.

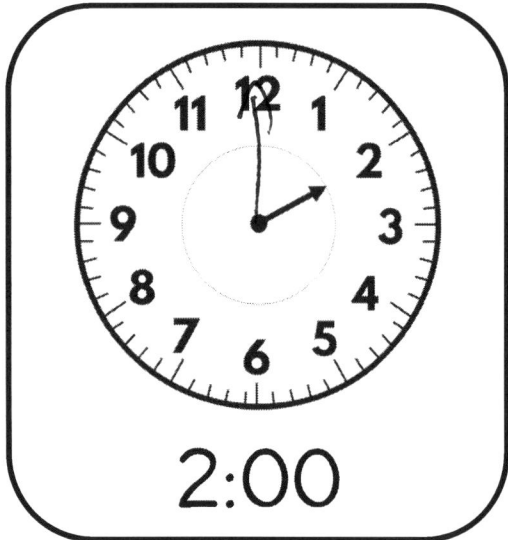

10:30

8:00

2:00

1:30

3:30

5:00

Let's Learn Quarter After

When the minute hand is on the 3, the time is 15 minutes after the hour. Other ways to say this are quarter after or quarter past the hour.

Below each clock is the matching digital time.

12:15

1:15

2:15

3:15

4:15

5:15

6:15

7:15

8:15

9:15

10:15

11:15

Trace and write the digital time and then trace the clock's minute hand.

12:15

1:15

2:15

Name: _____ Date: _____

Trace and write the digital time and then trace the clock's minute hand.

3:15

4:15

5:15

Name: _____ Date: _____

Trace and write the digital time and then trace the clock's minute hand.

6:15

7:15

8:15

Name:_____ Date:_____

Trace and write the digital time and then trace the clock's minute hand.

9:15

10:15

11:15

Write the digital time.

Answers to choose from:

4:15   1:15   5:15   12:15   2:15   3:15

Write the digital time.

_____
. . . .
_____

_____
. . . .
_____

_____
. . . .
_____

_____
. . . .
_____

_____
. . . .
_____

_____
. . . .
_____

Answers to choose from:

7:15   10:15   8:15   11:15   6:15   9:15

Name: ____________________ Date: ______________

Circle the correct clock for each digital time.

12:15

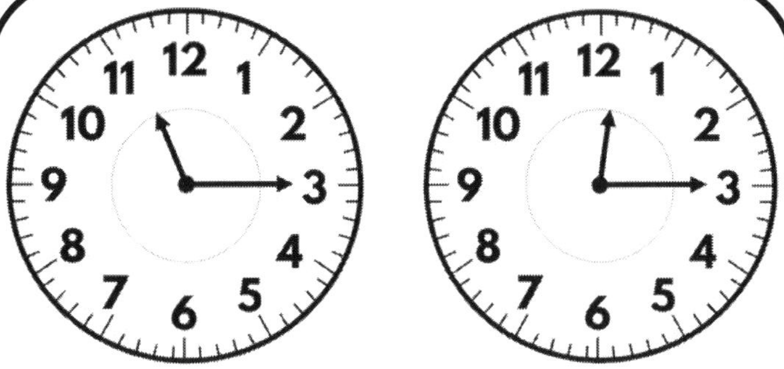

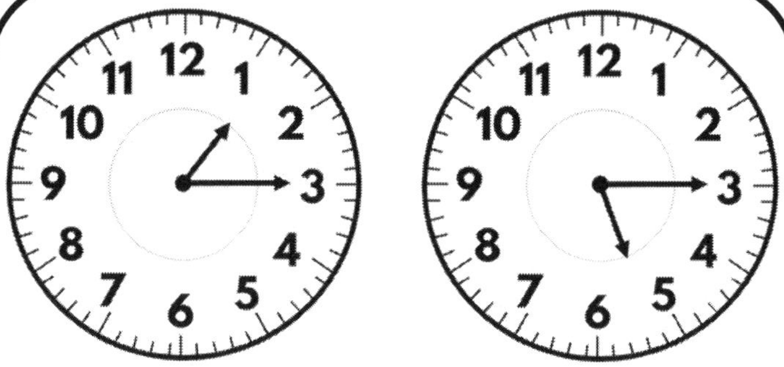

1:15

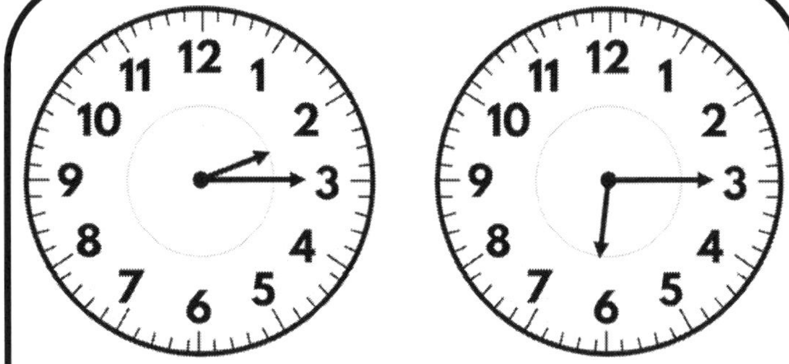

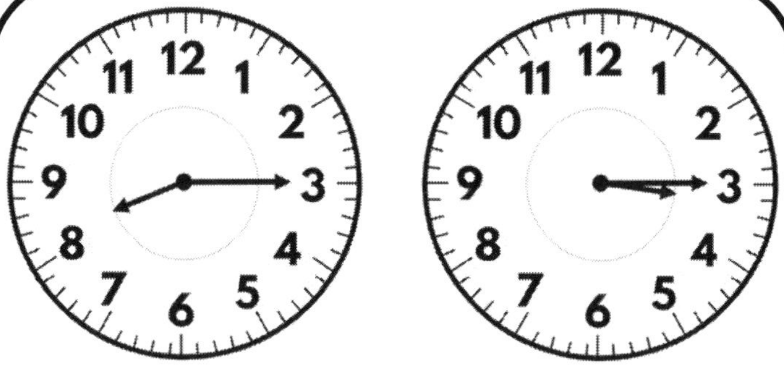

2:15

3:15

Name: _____ Date: _____

Circle the correct clock
for each digital time.

4:15

5:15

6:15

7:15

Name:_____ Date:_____

Circle the correct clock for each digital time.

8:15

9:15

10:15

11:15

Let's Learn Quarter To

When the minute hand is on the 9, the time is 45 minutes after the hour. Other ways to say this are quarter to, quarter of, or quarter until the hour.

Below each clock is the matching digital time.

12:45

1:45

2:45

3:45

4:45

5:45

6:45

7:45

8:45

9:45

10:45

11:45

Name:_____ Date:_____

Trace the clock's minute hand and then trace and write the digital time.

12:45

1:45

2:45

Trace the clock's minute hand and then trace and write the digital time.

Trace the clock's minute hand and then trace and write the digital time.

6:45

7:45

8:45

Name:_____ Date:_____

Trace the clock's minute hand and then trace and write the digital time.

Name:_____ Date:_____

Write the hour number for each clock. Practice tracing the quarter to time.

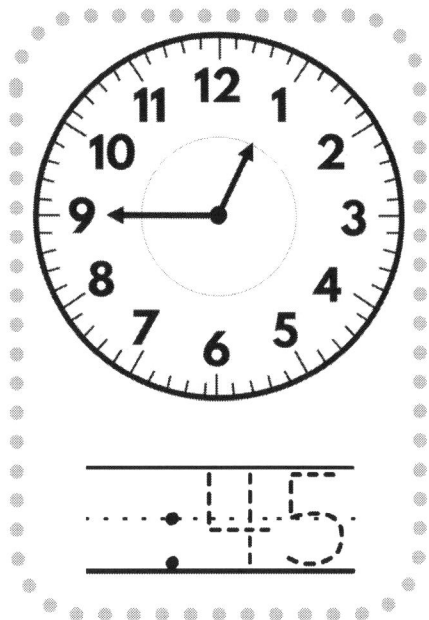

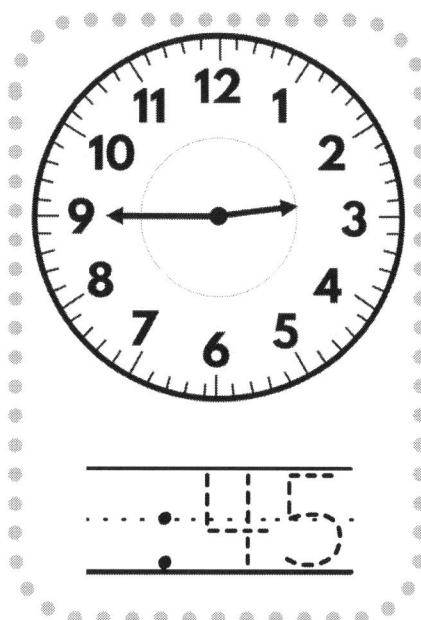

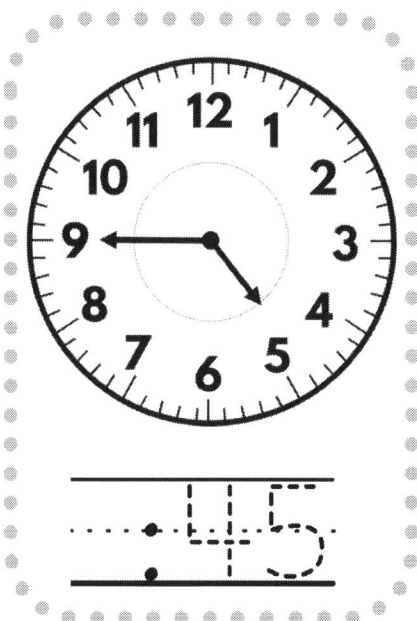

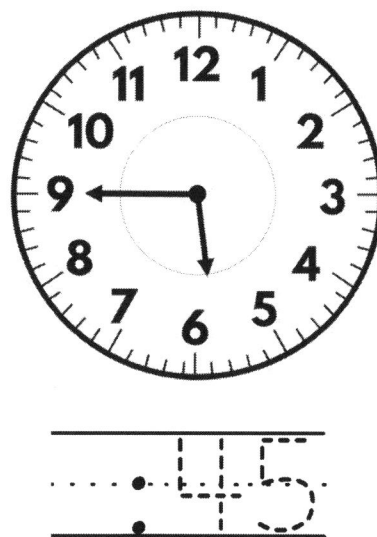

Name:_____ Date:_____

Write the hour number for each clock. Practice tracing the quarter to time.

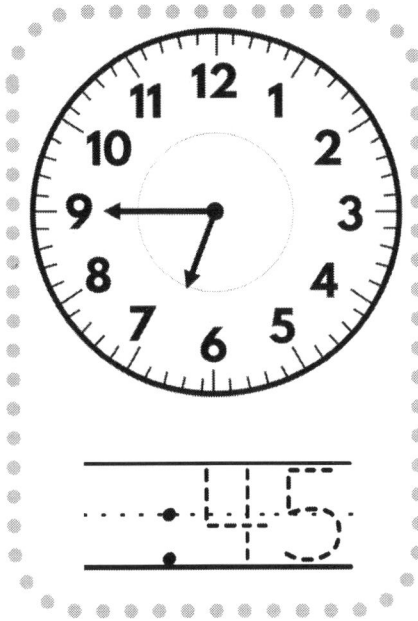

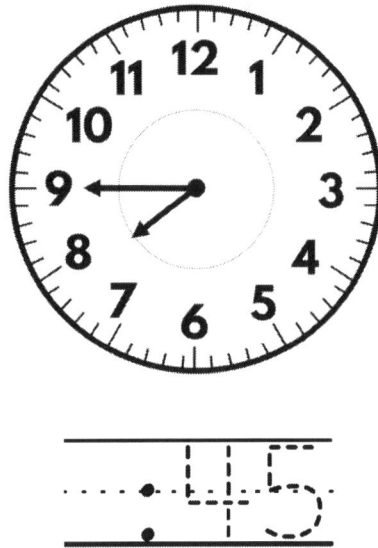

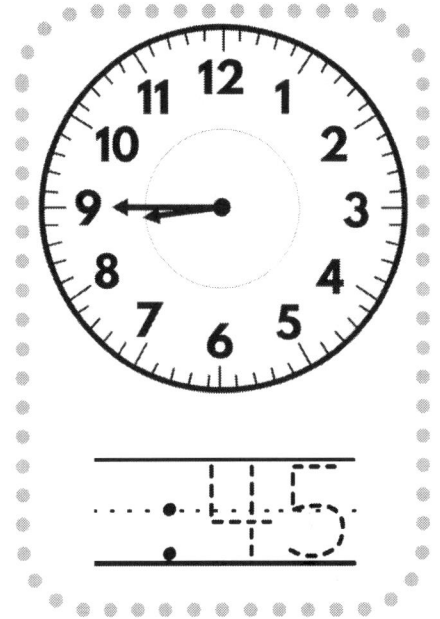

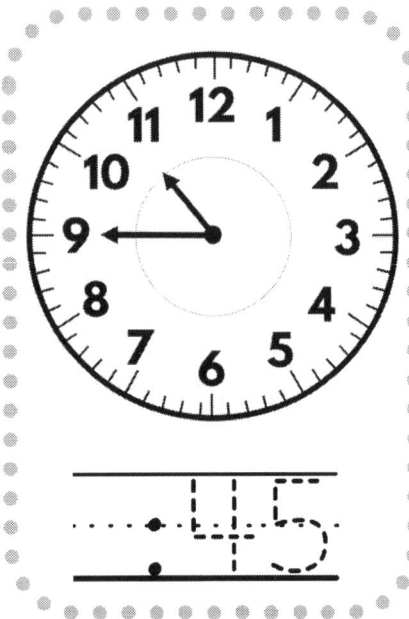

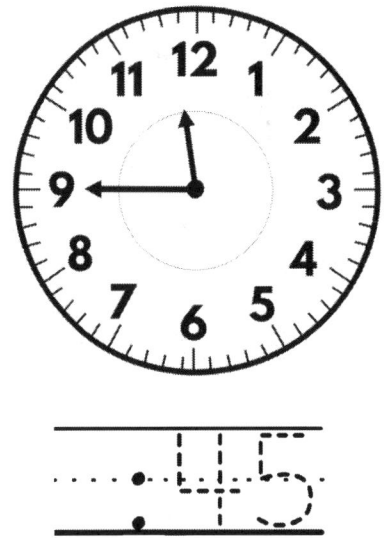

45   45   45

45   45   45

Name: Vivia   Date: _____

Circle the correct clock for each digital time.

12:45

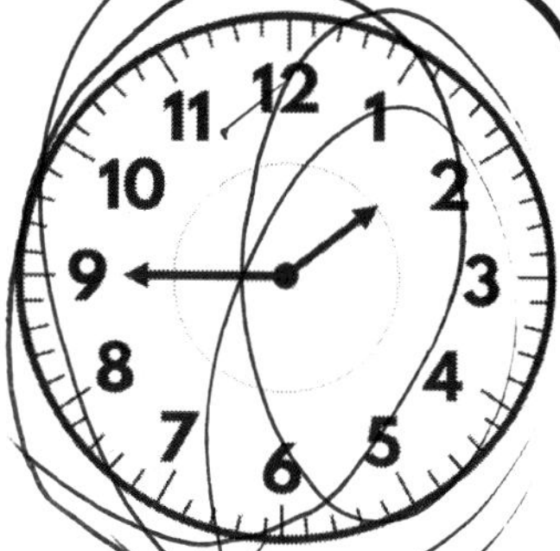

1:45

2:45

3:45

Name: ViVia   Date: _____

Circle the correct clock for each digital time.

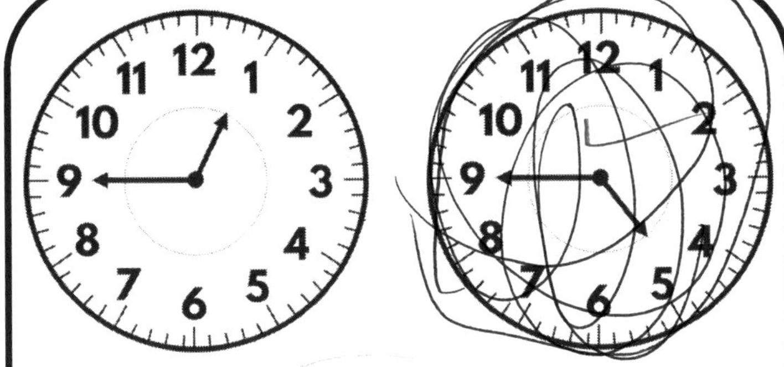

4:45

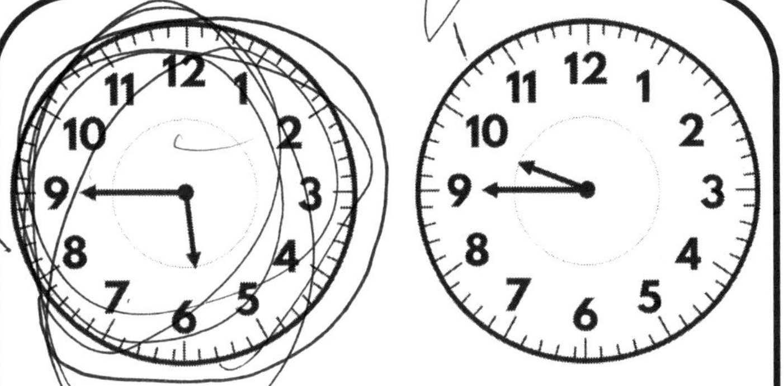

5:45

6:45

7:45

Circle the correct clock
for each digital time.

8:45

9:45

10:45

11:45

Name:_____ Date:_____

Connect the digital times as they move forward 15 minutes.

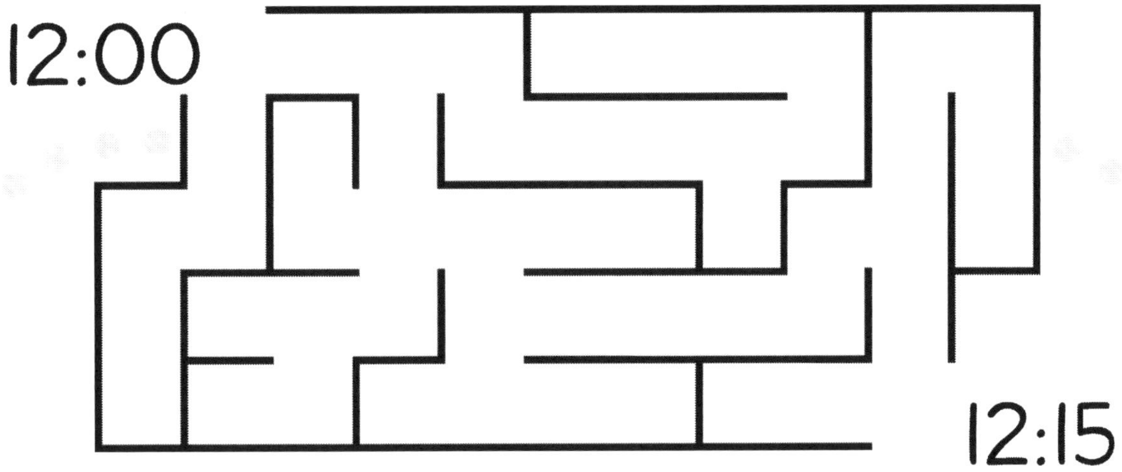

12:00

12:15

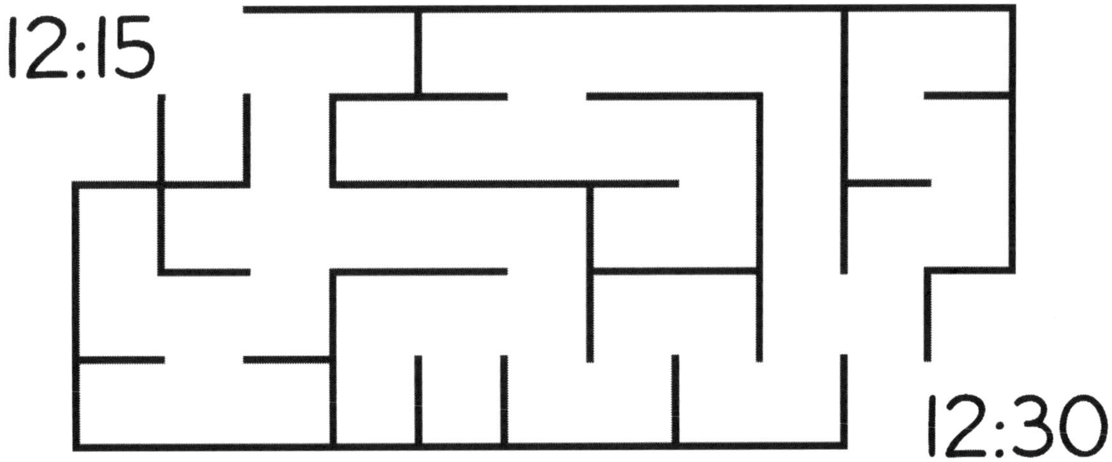

12:15

12:30

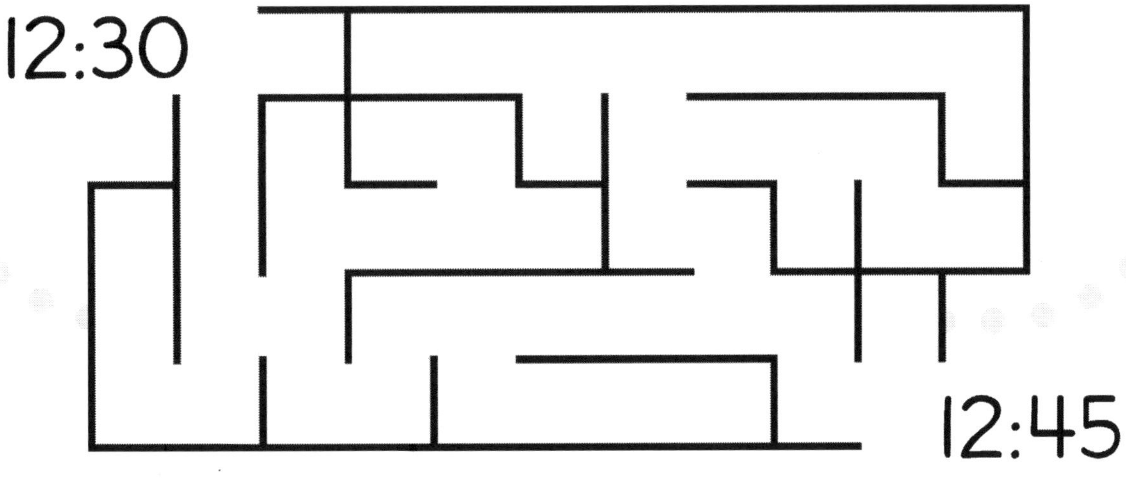

12:30

12:45

Name:_____ Date:_____

Connect the digital times as they move forward 15 minutes.

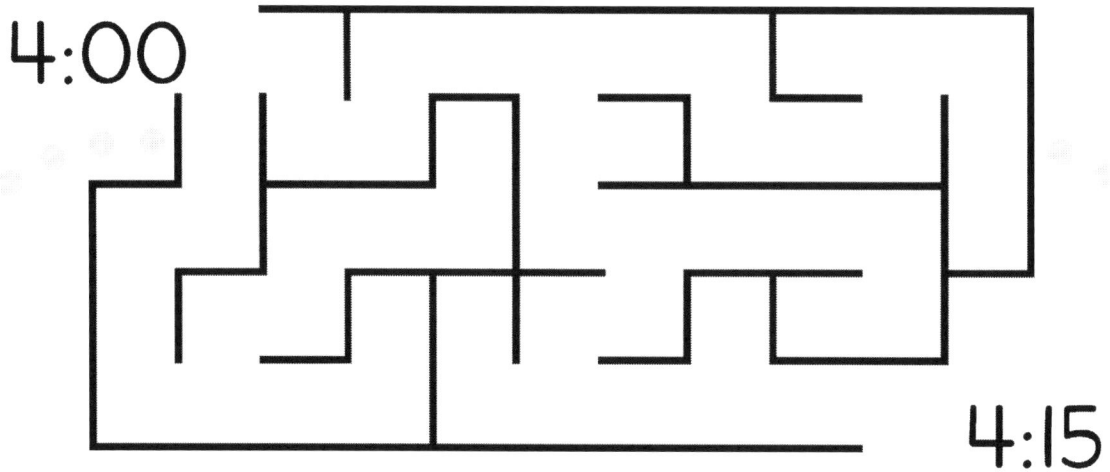

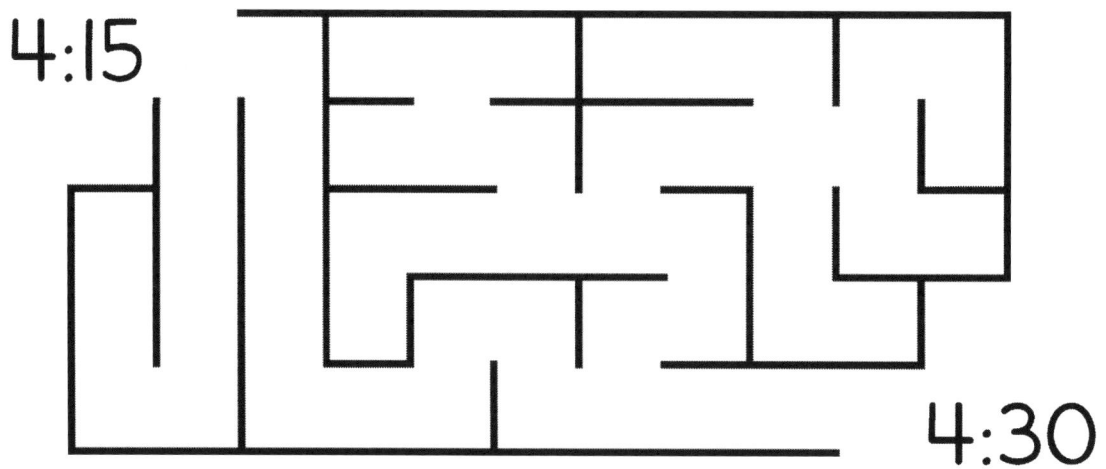

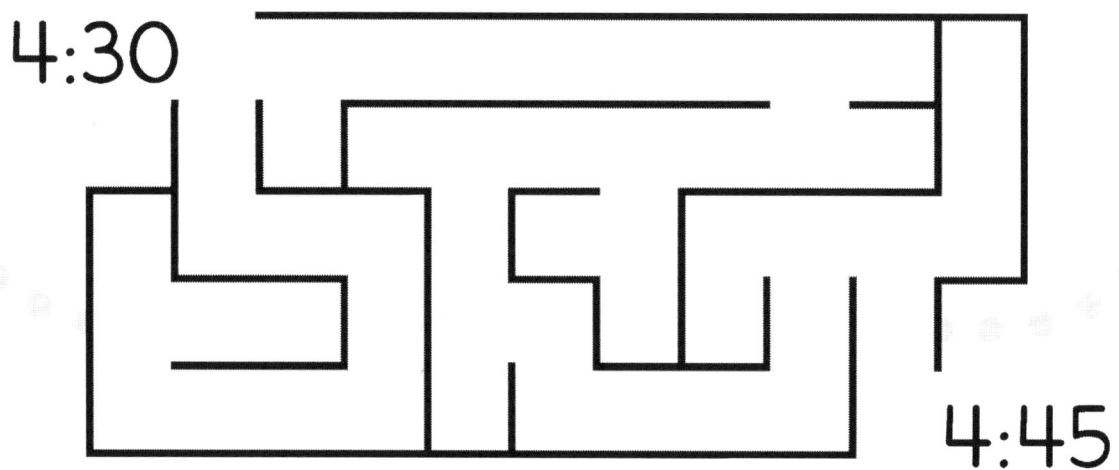

4:00

4:15

4:15

4:30

4:30

4:45

Name: _____ Date: _____

Connect the digital times as they move forward 15 minutes.

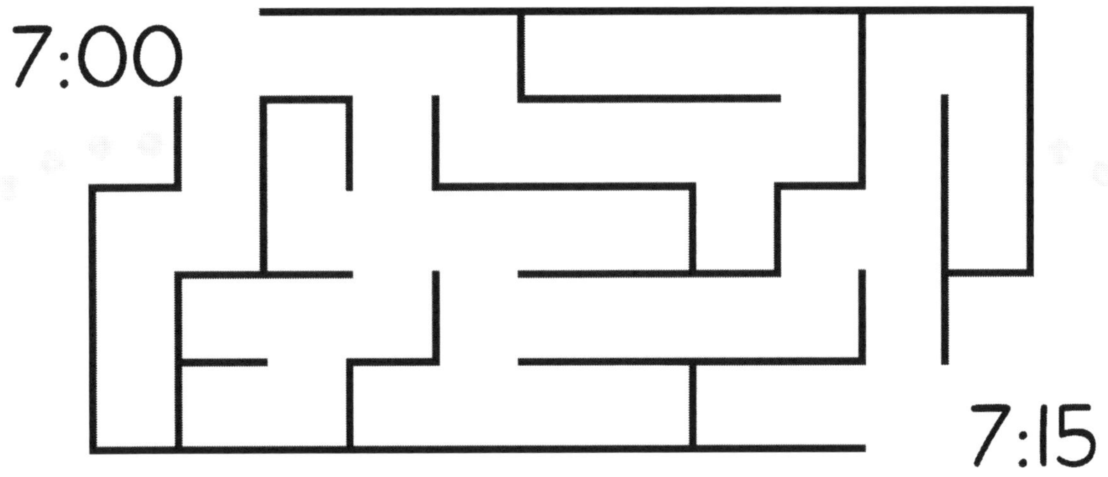

7:00

7:15

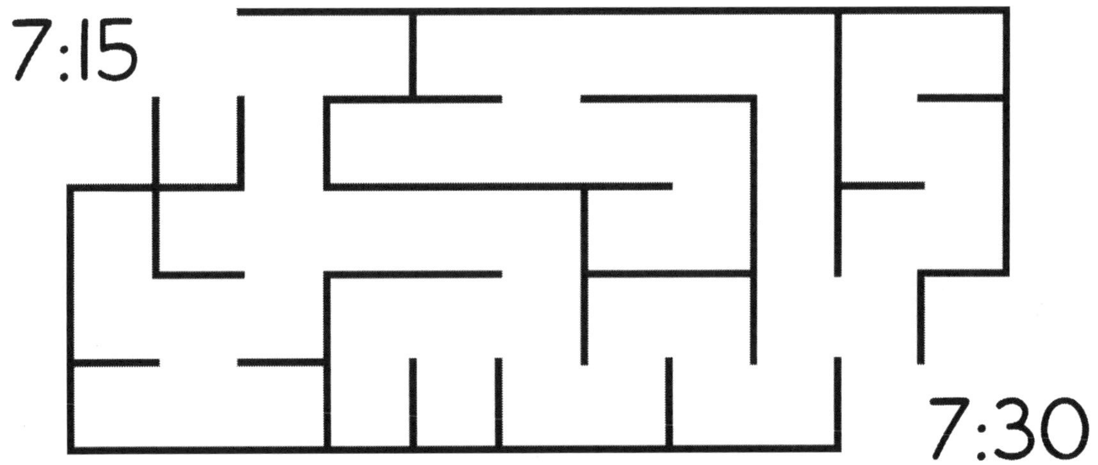

7:15

7:30

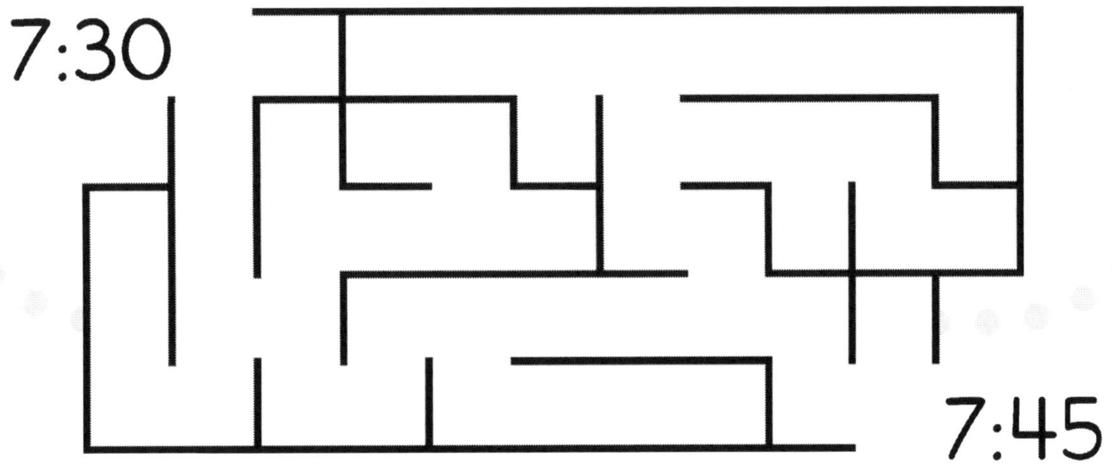

7:30

7:45

Name: _____ Date: _____

Connect the digital times as they move forward 15 minutes.

11:00

11:15

11:15

11:30

11:30

11:45

AM & PM Introduction

One day is made up of 24 hours.

The first twelve (12) hour period from midnight to noon is called a.m., which is short for "ante meridiem" in Latin. That means "before midday".

The second twelve (12) hour period is called p.m., which is short for "post meridiem". In Latin, that means "after midday".

When you eat breakfast at 8 o'clock in the morning, the time is 8 a.m.

When you go to bed at 8 o'clock in the evening, the time is 8 p.m.

When you put all the hours of a.m. and p.m. together, it equals one whole day!

Name: _____ Date: _____

G X K Z C X H A L F I N
T I M E W S W I R T I U
X T I N I G H T O G H M
P F A C E X K G D V W B
H M I G H R M O A B V E
O N N S T M Z G E U D R
U H A N D I M O Q C W V
R C O I M N V S A W Q G
D L D F P U B O B M J T
R O S A N T J G Q U H B
T C P D Y E R H G F K L
C K E C E I Y W H O N J

AM   HOUR
CLOCK   MINUTE
DAY   NIGHT
FACE   NUMBER
HALF   PM
HAND   TIME

Page 86

Let's Learn The Days of the Week

There are seven days in a week and each one has its own name. Starting at the beginning of the week, the days are:

Sunday
Monday
Tuesday
Wednesday
Thursday
Friday
Saturday

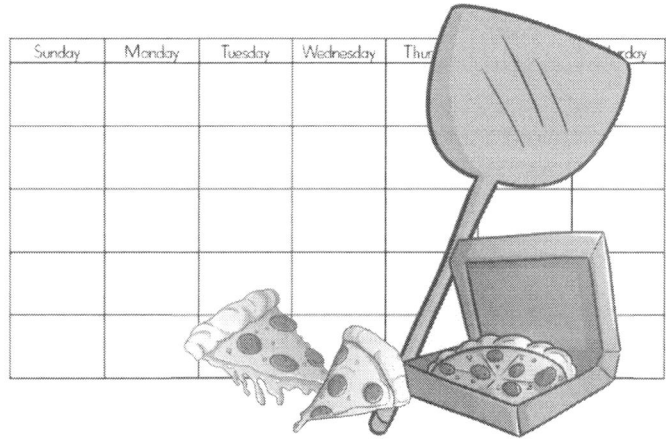

On a calendar, the days of the week will look like:

Sunday	Monday	Tuesday	Wednesday	Thursday	Friday	Saturday

Name:_____ Date:_____

Trace and write the day of the week.

Sunday

Sunday

Sunday

Draw a smiley face in each Sunday on the calendar. ☺

Sunday	Monday	Tuesday	Wednesday	Thursday	Friday	Saturday

Name: _____ Date: _____

Trace and write the day of the week.

Monday ···

Monday ···

Monday ···

Draw a smiley face in each Monday on the calendar. ☺

Sunday	Monday	Tuesday	Wednesday	Thursday	Friday	Saturday

Name:_____ Date:_____

Trace and write the day of the week.

Tuesday

Tuesday

Tuesday

Draw a smiley face in each Tuesday on the calendar. ☺

Sunday	Monday	Tuesday	Wednesday	Thursday	Friday	Saturday

Name: _____ Date: _____

Trace and write the day of the week.

Wednesday

Wednesday

Wednesday

Draw a smiley face in each Wednesday on the calendar. ☺

Sunday	Monday	Tuesday	Wednesday	Thursday	Friday	Saturday

Name:_____ Date:_____

Trace and write the day of the week.

Thursday

Thursday

Thursday

Draw a smiley face in each Thursday on the calendar. ☺

Sunday	Monday	Tuesday	Wednesday	Thursday	Friday	Saturday

Name:_____ Date:_____

Trace and write the day of the week.

Friday

Friday

Friday

Draw a smiley face in each Friday on the calendar. ☺

Sunday	Monday	Tuesday	Wednesday	Thursday	Friday	Saturday

Name: _____ Date: _____

Trace and write the day of the week.

Saturday

Saturday

Saturday

Draw a smiley face in each Saturday on the calendar. ☺

Sunday	Monday	Tuesday	Wednesday	Thursday	Friday	Saturday

Name: _____ Date: _____

Yesterday is the day before today.
Today is the present day.
Tomorrow is the day after today.

Practice tracing and writing each word.

yesterday

today

tomorrow

Practice writing the day of the week for today, yesterday, and tomorrow.

Today is

Yesterday was

Tomorrow will be

Let's Learn The Months of the Year

There are twelve months in a year and each one has its own name. Starting at the beginning of the year, the months are:

January (1)

February (2)

March (3)

April (4)

May (5)

June (6)

July (7)

August (8)

September (9)

October (10)

November (11)

December (12)

Sunday	Monday	Tuesday	Wednesday	Thursday	Friday	Saturday

On a calendar, the month will be on the top and might look like:

January

Sunday	Monday	Tuesday	Wednesday	Thursday	Friday	Saturday

Name: _____ Date: _____

Practice tracing and writing the months.

January _____

February _____

March _____

April _____

May _____

June _____

Name:_____ Date:_____

Practice tracing and writing the months.

July

August

September

October

November

December

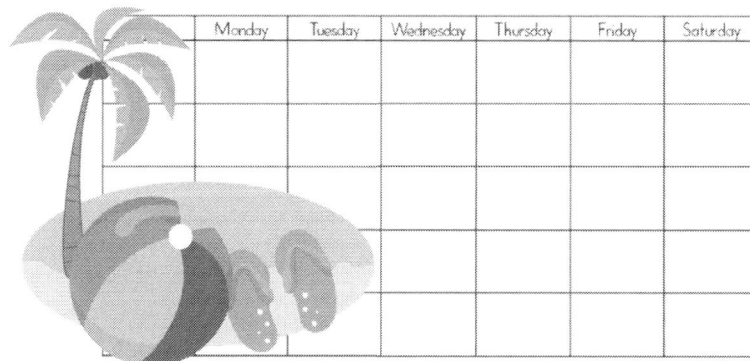

	Monday	Tuesday	Wednesday	Thursday	Friday	Saturday

Name:_____ Date:_____

Each month can have up to 31 days.
Practice tracing the numbers one to thirty-one.

1   2   3   4   5   6

7   8   9   10   11   12

13   14   15   16   17

18   19   20   21   22

23   24   25   26   27

28   29   30   31

January

January is the first month in the calendar year and has 31 days.

Write the month and year on the blank line then color in the picture.
(Have an adult help you fill in the calendar numbers.)

_____

. . . .

Sunday	Monday	Tuesday	Wednesday	Thursday	Friday	Saturday

Name: _____ Date: _____

February

February is the second month in the calendar year and normally has 28 days – except on a leap year and then it has 29 days.

Write the month and year on the blank line.
(Have an adult help you fill in the calendar numbers.)

_____

· ·

_____

Sunday	Monday	Tuesday	Wednesday	Thursday	Friday	Saturday

Name: _____ Date: _____

March

March is the third month in the calendar year and has 31 days.

Write the month and year on the blank line.
(Have an adult help you fill in the calendar numbers.)

_____

. . . .

Sunday	Monday	Tuesday	Wednesday	Thursday	Friday	Saturday

Name: _____ Date: _____

April

April is the fourth month in the calendar year and has 30 days.

Write the month and year on the blank line.
(Have an adult help you fill in the calendar numbers.)

_____

. . . .

_____

Sunday	Monday	Tuesday	Wednesday	Thursday	Friday	Saturday

Name: _____ Date: _____

May

May is the fifth month in the calendar year and has 31 days.

Write the month and year on the blank line.
(Have an adult help you fill in the calendar numbers.)

_____
. . . .

Sunday	Monday	Tuesday	Wednesday	Thursday	Friday	Saturday

Name: _____ Date: _____

June

June is the sixth month in the calendar year and has 30 days.

Write the month and year on the blank line.
(Have an adult help you fill in the calendar numbers.)

_____

· ·

_____

Sunday	Monday	Tuesday	Wednesday	Thursday	Friday	Saturday

Name: _____ Date: _____

July

July is the seventh month in the calendar year and has 31 days.

Write the month and year on the blank line.
(Have an adult help you fill in the calendar numbers.)

_____

. . . .

Sunday	Monday	Tuesday	Wednesday	Thursday	Friday	Saturday

Name: _____ Date: _____

August

August is the eighth month in the calendar year and has 31 days.

Write the month and year on the blank line.
(Have an adult help you fill in the calendar numbers.)

_____
. . . .
_____

Sunday	Monday	Tuesday	Wednesday	Thursday	Friday	Saturday

Name: _____ Date: _____

September

September is the ninth month in the calendar year and has 30 days.

Write the month and year on the blank line.
(Have an adult help you fill in the calendar numbers.)

_____

. . . .

Sunday	Monday	Tuesday	Wednesday	Thursday	Friday	Saturday

Name:_____ Date:_____

October

October is the tenth month in the calendar year and has 31 days.

Write the month and year on the blank line.
(Have an adult help you fill in the calendar numbers.)

_____

. . . .

_____

Sunday	Monday	Tuesday	Wednesday	Thursday	Friday	Saturday

Name: _____ Date: _____

November

November is the eleventh month in the calendar year and has 30 days.

Write the month and year on the blank line.
(Have an adult help you fill in the calendar numbers.)

_____

. . . .

Sunday	Monday	Tuesday	Wednesday	Thursday	Friday	Saturday

Name: _____ Date: _____

December

December is the twelfth month in the calendar year and has 31 days.

Write the month and year on the blank line.
(Have an adult help you fill in the calendar numbers.)

_____

. . . .

_____

Sunday	Monday	Tuesday	Wednesday	Thursday	Friday	Saturday

Name: _____ Date: _____

Some holidays fall on the same day every year. Some special days change from year to year, like the first day of summer.

On the calendars you just made, circle the following holidays and put a check mark in the box when done.

☐ New Year's Day – January 1

☐ Valentine's Day – February 14

☐ Halloween – October 31

Other ideas for days to circle on your calendar:

☐ Your birthday

☐ First days of spring, summer, fall and winter

☐ First day of school, last day of school

☐ Thanksgiving

☐ Winter holidays and celebrations

Name: _____ Date: _____

There are 12 hours on a clock face.
Practice tracing and writing the numbers.

1   2

3   4

5   6

7   8

9   10

11   12

Practice tracing and writing the digital time for each hour.

1:00   2:00   3:00

4:00   5:00   6:00

7:00   8:00   9:00

10:00   11:00   12:00

Name:_____ Date:_____

Practice writing the digital time for each hour.

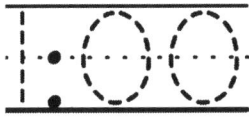

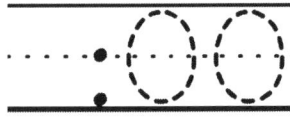

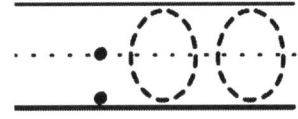

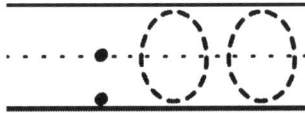

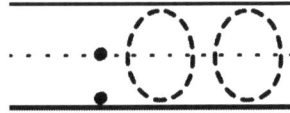

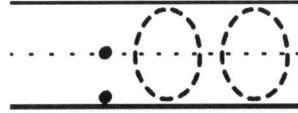

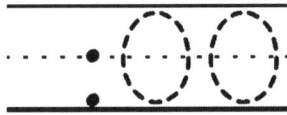

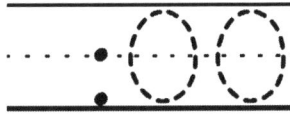

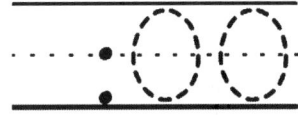

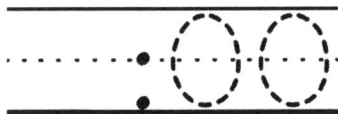

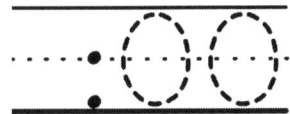

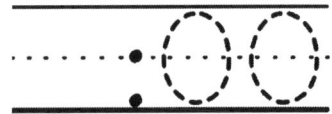

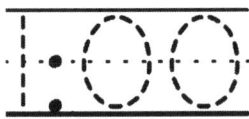

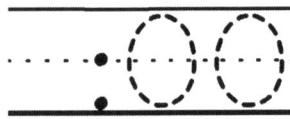

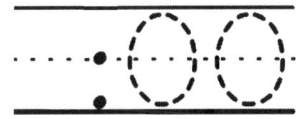

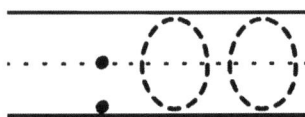

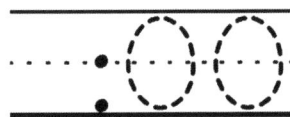

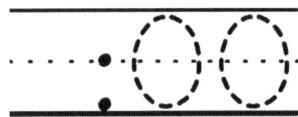

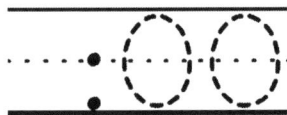

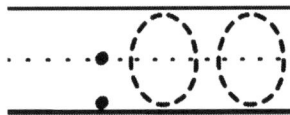

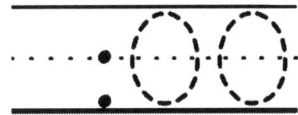

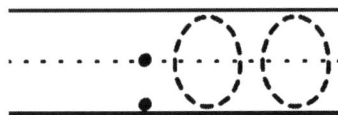

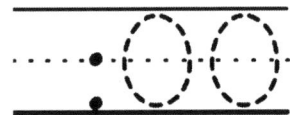

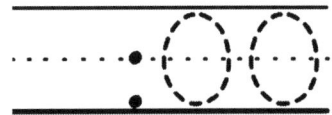

Name:_____ Date:_____

Practice writing the number words one to six.

One

Two

Three

Four

Five

Six

Name: _____ Date: _____

Practice writing the number words seven to twelve.

Seven

Eight

Nine

Ten

Eleven

Twelve

Practice tracing the number words.

1

2

One

Two

3

4

Three

Four

5

6

Five

Six

Name:_____ Date:_____

Practice tracing the number words.

7   8

Seven   Eight

9   10

Nine   Ten

11   12

Eleven   Twelve

Answer Keys and Solutions

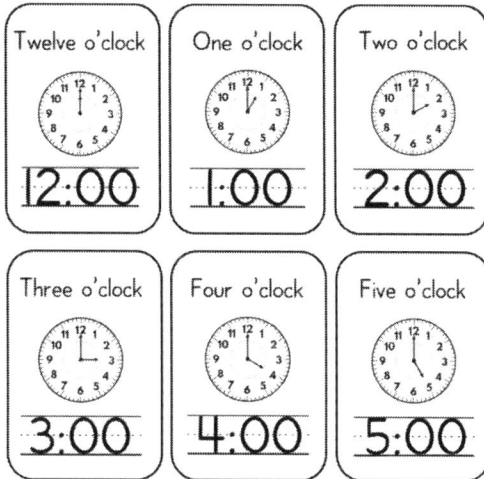

Page 17

Page 18

Page 19

Page 20

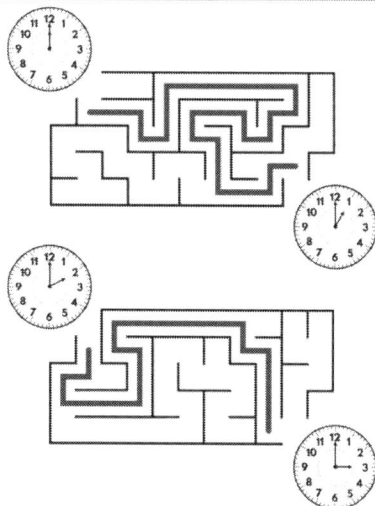

Page 21

Page 22

Answer Keys and Solutions

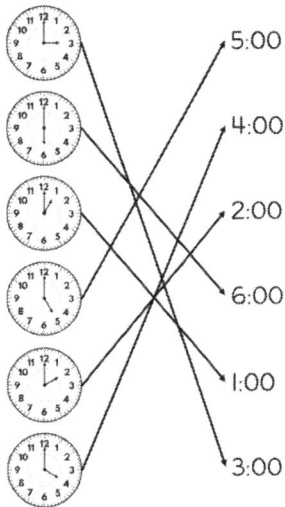

Page 25

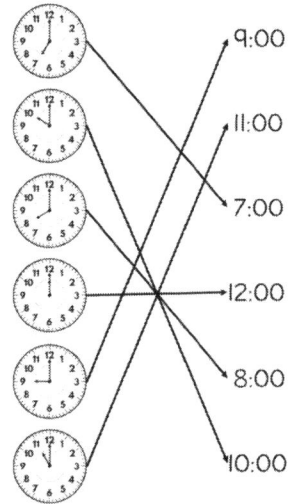

Page 26

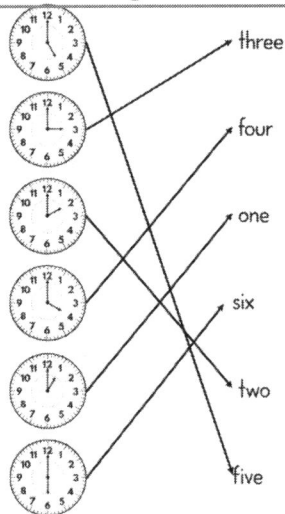

Page 27

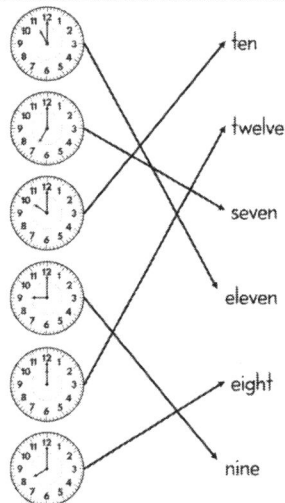

Page 28

Page 29

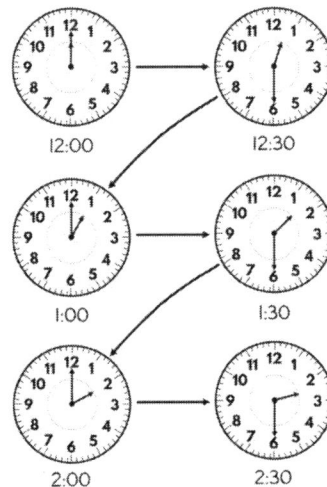

Page 43

Answer Keys and Solutions

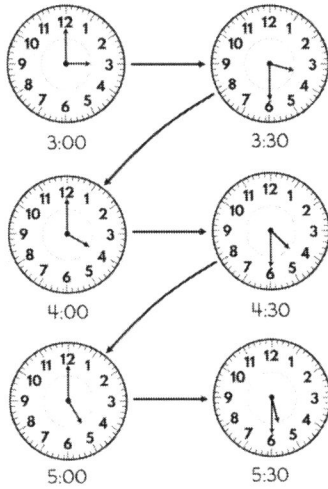

Page 44

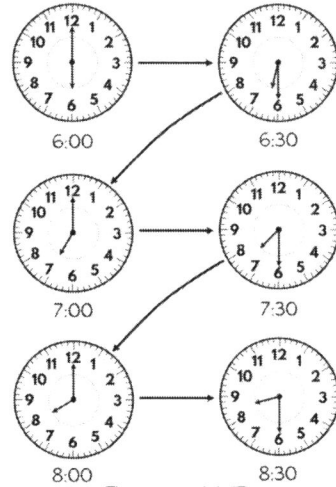

Page 45

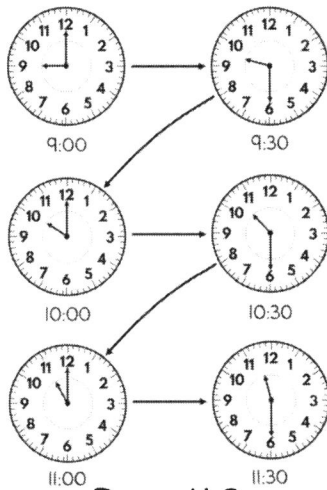

Page 46

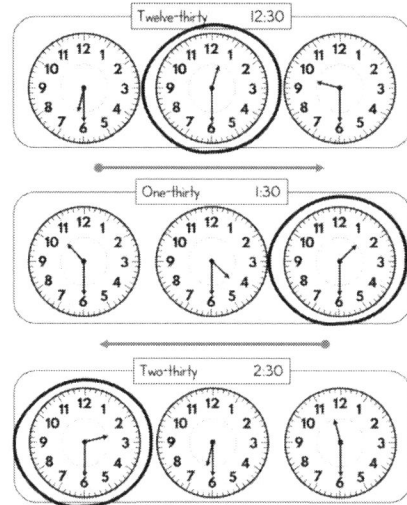

Page 50

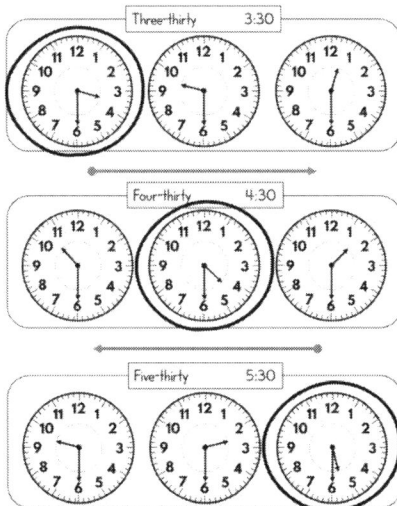

Page 51

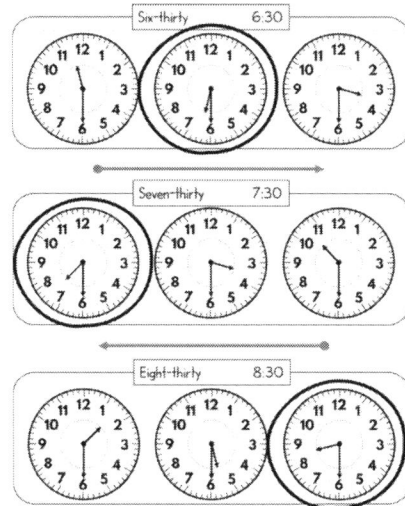

Page 52

Answer Keys and Solutions

Nine-thirty 9:30

Ten-thirty 10:30

Eleven-thirty 11:30

Page 53

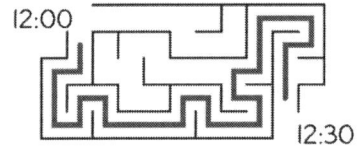

12:00 — 12:30

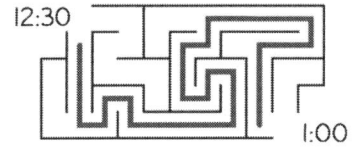

12:30 — 1:00

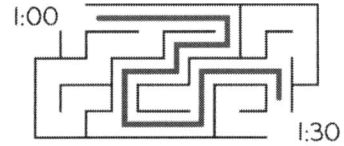

1:00 — 1:30

Page 54

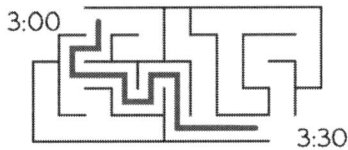

3:00 — 3:30

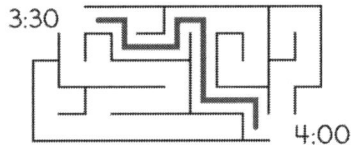

3:30 — 4:00

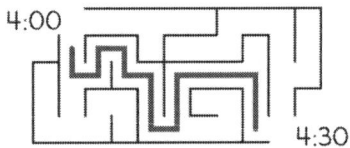

4:00 — 4:30

Page 55

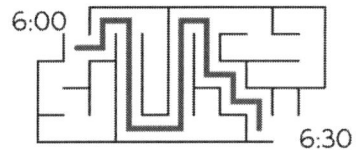

6:00 — 6:30

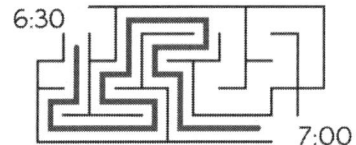

6:30 — 7:00

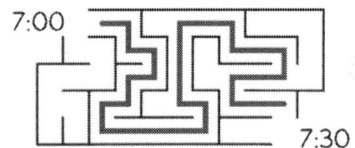

7:00 — 7:30

Page 56

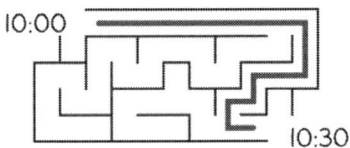

10:00 — 10:30

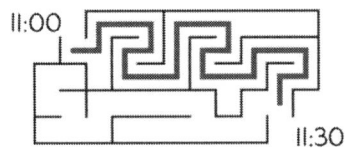

11:00 — 11:30

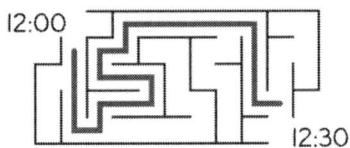

12:00 — 12:30

Page 57

 12:00
 4:30
 7:30
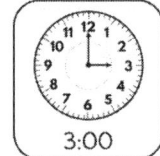 3:00
 11:00
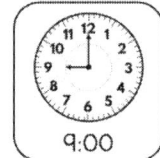 9:00

Page 58

Answer Keys and Solutions

2:30   8:30

6:00   1:00

5:30   9:30

Page 59

10:30   8:00

2:00   1:30

3:30   5:00

Page 60

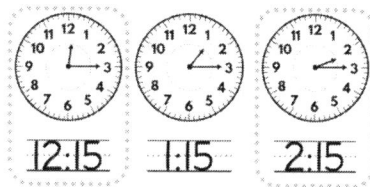

12:15   1:15   2:15

3:15   4:15   5:15

Page 66

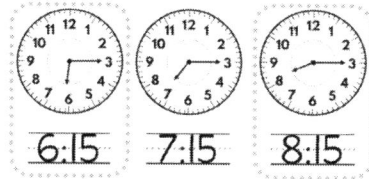

6:15   7:15   8:15

9:15   10:15   11:15

Page 67

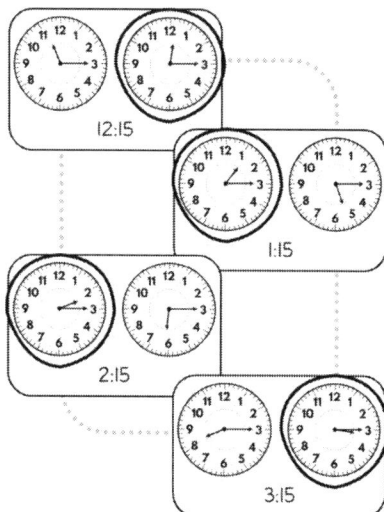

12:15

1:15

2:15

3:15

Page 68

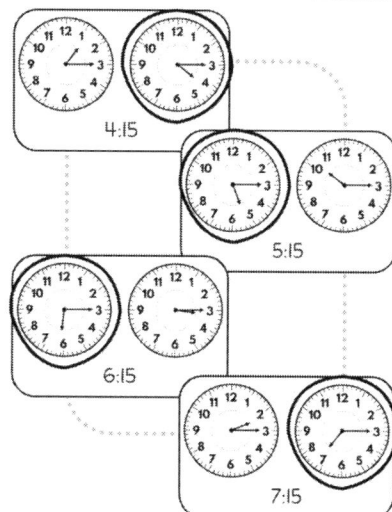

4:15

5:15

6:15

7:15

Page 69

Answer Keys and Solutions

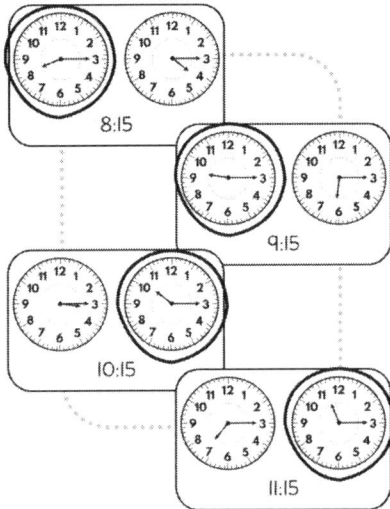

8:15
9:15
10:15
11:15

Page 70

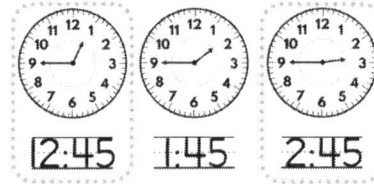

12:45   1:45   2:45

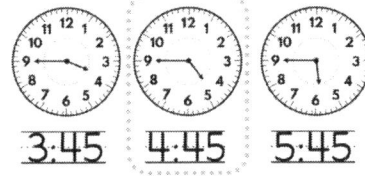

3:45   4:45   5:45

Page 76

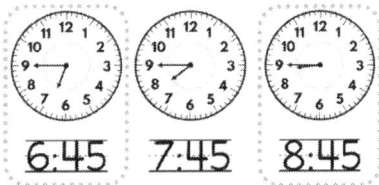

6:45   7:45   8:45

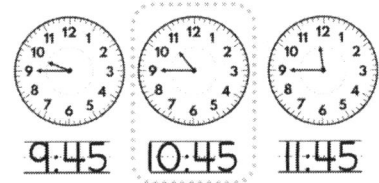

9:45   10:45   11:45

Page 77

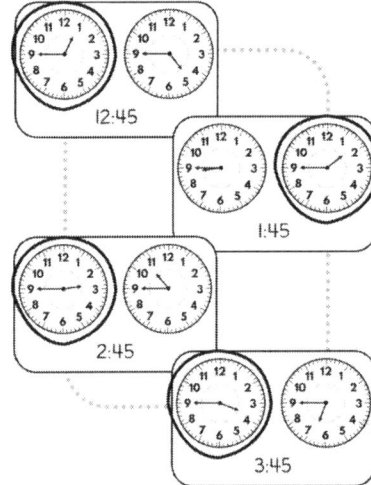

12:45
1:45
2:45
3:45

Page 78

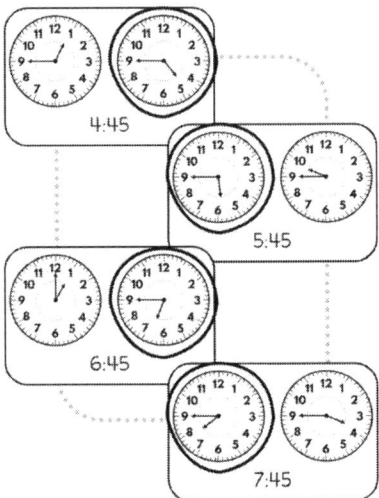

4:45
5:45
6:45
7:45

Page 79

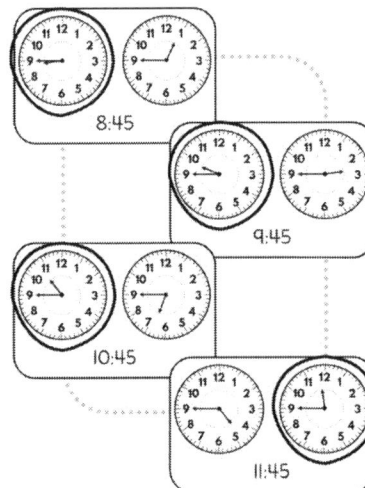

8:45
9:45
10:45
11:45

Page 80

Answer Keys and Solutions

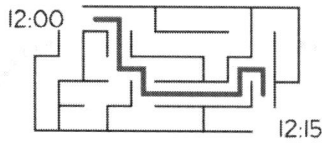

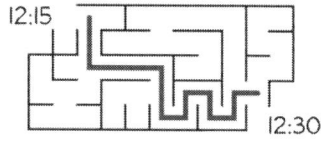

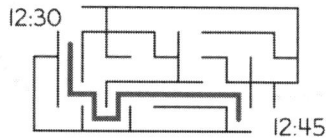

Page 81

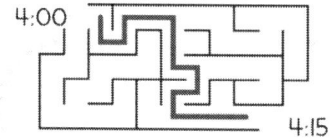

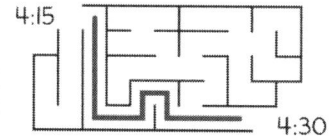

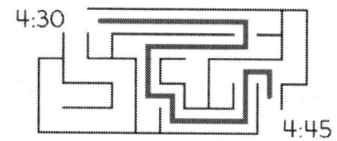

Page 82

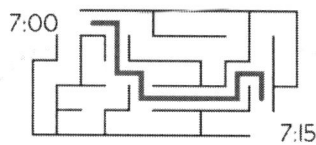

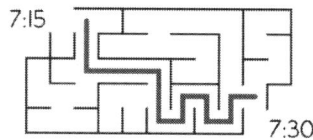

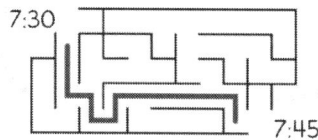

Page 83

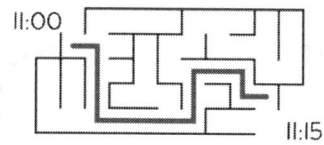

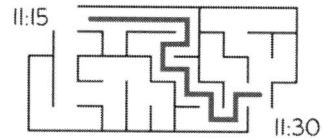

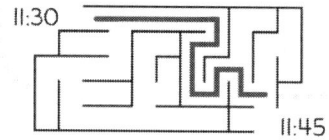

Page 84

Page 86

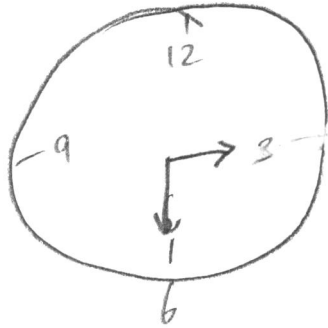

14529904R00070